PERSONALITY NEGOTIATING

Conflict
Without
Casualty

TOM ANASTASI

D0104147

Sterling Publishing Co., Inc. New York

To
my grandparents
Thomas and Catherine Anastasi

Personality Selling is a registered trademark and servicemark
of Sales and Negotiating Training Company.
Personality Negotiating is a trademark and servicemark of Sales
and Negotiating Training Company.

Library of Congress Cataloging-in-Publication Data
Anastasi, Thomas E.
    Personality negotiating : conflict without casualty / Tom
Anastasi.
        p.   cm.
    Includes bibliographical references and index.
    ISBN 0-8069-8537-2
    1. Negotiation.   2. Personality.   I. Title
BF637.N4A48   1993
158'.5—dc20   92-36154
                                                            CIP

10 9 8 7 6 5 4 3 2 1

Edited by Claire Bazinet

Published in 1993 by Sterling Publishing Company, Inc.
387 Park Avenue South, New York, NY 10016
© 1993 by Tom Anastasi
Distributed in Canada by Sterling Publishing
% Canadian Manda Group, P.O. Box 920, Station U
Toronto, Ontario, Canada M8Z 5P9
Distributed in Great Britain and Europe by Cassell PLC
Villiers House, 41/47 Strand, London WC2N 5JE, England
Distributed in Australia by Capricorn Link Ltd.
P.O. Box 665, Lane Cove, NSW 2066
Manufactured in the United States of America
All rights reserved

Sterling ISBN 0-8069-8537-2

CONTENTS

PREFACE

What led to the birth of this sequel to my book *Personality Selling*? After piling up the frequent-flyer miles crisscrossing the country doing Personality Selling® seminars, I was often asked to do the seminar for non-salespeople. What I quickly found out is that many people are familiar with the principles and mechanics of negotiation, but not how to negotiate with living human beings.

The five billion, or so, of us in the world are all unique. Yet, we share traits that are similar to some, and different from others. The variation on the theme of personhood is wonderful, confusing, and at times, frightening.

Personality Negotiating™ works because it, too, is different. The one thing I've found in several years' experience in negotiating is that no two negotiations are ever alike. That's why learning only one way to negotiate puts you at a disadvantage. It only works for people who fit that one specific mould—and they are few and very far between. After you finish this book, you'll be able to come up with collaborative solutions with all types of people in all types of negotiations—I promise. And the best part is that you can just be yourself.

Good luck and good negotiating!

Tom Anastasi

Chapter 1
HOW PERSONALITY NEGOTIATING WORKS

Business is one big negotiation. We all spend a good part of our day negotiating with coworkers, our bosses, other departments, customers, suppliers, and salespeople. Today, more than ever, resources are scarce, budgets are tight, and people everywhere want their fair share of the pie. With Personality Negotiating, the marriage of negotiation skills and psychology, you'll know how to negotiate with all types of people in all types of situations.

Using Personality Negotiating, problems get solved collaboratively yielding results that are optimal for everyone involved. Because everyone is a winner, relationships are not only preserved, they're enhanced. Without Personality Negotiating, the pie isn't always fairly divided. This can lead to animosity, the breakdown of communication, and the destruction of valuable relationships.

Personality Negotiating is a behavioral approach to negotiating that enables you to use your natural communication and observation abilities to better understand others' negotiating styles. You do this by discovering and keying in on your personality traits and those of the people you're negotiating with. Understanding how these personality traits influence behavior lets you adapt your negotiating style to theirs. The result is that you'll both find dealing with each other easier and more fruitful. The agreements you walk away with will be the best they can be for everyone.

Some People Are Easier to Deal With

Have you wondered why some people are naturally much easier to negotiate with than others? The reason is that people with personalities similar to yours see things as you do, so your styles merge and communication flows easily. You deal with them as they want to be dealt with, and vice versa. Those who don't share your personality traits see things differently, so without Personality Negotiating, you have to work harder to get your message through and to appreciate what they're saying. With Personality Negotiating, you can discover these different traits and modify your approach accordingly. Even when you and others have different personalities and different agendas, your negotiation style will click with theirs. Everyone is potentially easy to negotiate with. Personality Negotiating makes that potential a reality for you.

Personality Negotiating Is Not a Tug-of-War

Not only is Personality Negotiating different from a battle of wills, it is the antithesis of a battle. In a battle, the idea is to get as much as you can, while giving up as little as possible. In general terms, in a battle you have three possible outcomes: 1) a clear winner and a clear loser; 2) a draw; or 3) two losers. In every case, someone walks away unhappy or unsatisfied.

With Personality Negotiating Both Walk Away Winners

One of the biggest negotiation myths is that negotiation is the art of compromise. When you use the Personality Negotiating principles you'll seldom need to compromise. This is because the vast majority of the time, parties can invent a solution that fully benefits all. Instead of maybe dividing the pie, you think up ways to make two pies.

You and the other side accomplish this by finding out what each of you needs and by giving up what you both can to get it. The ingredients to a successful negotiation are knowing what each other wants and developing strategies for change that will benefit everyone. You both walk away from the deal better off than when you started.

What's the Catch?

In most negotiations, achieving mutually beneficial agreements proceeds smoothly. This type of agreement is easy—assuming that those involved: 1) verbalize their desires; 2) want to listen; 3) understand and appreciate each other; and 4) desire and develop collaborative solutions. The catch is that everyone is not always a motivated negotiator; that is, don't want a mutually beneficial agreement. There are many reasons this occurs. The two most common are: 1) they want a deal that only benefits them; or 2) they would rather avoid any kind of conflict than negotiate.

Personality Negotiating shows you how to deal with motivated and the non-motivated negotiators.

Here's an example of how Personality Negotiating works:

Peter is the general manager for a sporting goods store at a summer resort. Each year his employees leave two weeks before Labor Day, his busiest time, to have a vacation before they go back to college.

Peter's policy is that students who leave before Labor Day will not be rehired the following summer.

The problem is that he rarely gets return help, and training new hires takes a long time. The employees like working at the store and would find it hard to get another job, but feel they need the time off before the start of the school year.

THE NEGOTIATION: Both Peter and the students know intuitively that the situation is a lose–lose deal, but no one has been able to break the impasse. However, using Personality Negotiating, the students have learned that basing arguments on how they *feel* would sway some people, but not Peter.

They know they must present Peter with factual evidence to change the rules. They must also devise a feasible implementation plan.

THE SOLUTION: The students' need is to have a vacation during the summer. Peter's need is to have coverage during Labor Day and return help the following year.

The solution is to have the employees take their vacations earlier in the summer and work through until Labor Day. They develop a plan showing how the schedules work with their vacations. Peter accepts the deal and everyone is satisfied.

Solutions Don't Always Jump Out at You

Collaborative solutions are not always this easy to reach. If they were, books like this wouldn't be necessary. Reaching mutually beneficial options is often possible because both parties have needs to be addressed and resources that can be spared. Sometimes that resource is money, other times it's effort, or accommodation. Sometimes the answer is straightforward and sometimes it's esoteric. Every negotiation isn't tortuous, but for the ones that are, Personality Negotiating channels your efforts to useful and practical goals.

The Good, the Bad, and the Ugly

Personality Negotiating provides practical and proven strategies for dealing with all types of negotiators—the good, the bad, and the ugly. You'll see all types and must deal with them regularly. Here are some examples:

Diane is going to be a bridesmaid at a friend's wedding on Sunday. She has to leave work promptly at 5:00 on Friday to attend the rehearsal. At 4:30, her boss gives her a lengthy report to finish by the end of the day.

Diane feels stress because she is being pulled in two directions. At 4:45 Diane knows that she can't finish the report in time. She approaches her boss with the problem. Here's how the good, the bad, and the ugly negotiating boss would react.

THE GOOD NEGOTIATING BOSS: I just got this task from my supervisor, who needs the report for the stockholders' meeting Monday at 10:00. Could you finish it early Monday morning? That way, you could go to the rehearsal, enjoy the weekend, and my boss could get her report.

She is a good negotiator because she seeks to address what's important to others, and then discuss what's significant to her. She works to invent situations that work for everyone.

STRATEGY: First, explain all the things that are important to you. Then, make sure that you have a complete grasp of the boss' concerns. Finally, develop a collaborative deal that works for both of you.

THE BAD NEGOTIATING BOSS: I know it's an inconvenience, but I just don't want to deal with this now. If you finish it today, we'll know it's done. So why don't you stay an hour to wrap it up?

This person is a bad negotiator, not because she is hostile, but because she wants to avoid conflict. Ironically, while trying to avoid conflict she creates new conflict.

COPING STRATEGY: First, empathize with bad negotiators, showing them you empathize that this conflict has put them in a difficult position. Then, explain the problem in impersonal terms. Finally, find out what their worst-case scenario is, and develop a scenario that will be amenable to them.

In this case, Diane's boss' worry is that the report won't get done by Monday. Diane assuages that fear by laying out a game plan that will keep to everyone's schedules.

DIANE: I'll work on the report tonight, after the rehearsal. If I have any problems, I'll give you a call. Sunday, after the wedding, I'll put it into the computer and it will be all set first thing Monday. Your supervisor won't have a chance to look at it by then, anyway.

The next type of negotiator is the ugly negotiator. Ugly negotiators don't care about the other party's needs. They care solely about their own.

> **THE UGLY NEGOTIATING BOSS:** If you leave before finishing the report, you're fired.

Ugly negotiators are difficult to deal with during any type of contact, including during negotiations. Fortunately, they can be managed. Here's what to do: 1) understand that the reason they are being belligerent is that they are insecure and feel threatened; 2) remember that escalating conflicts tend to threaten them; 3) defuse the anger by getting them to calm down; and 4) after they are calm, begin exploring alternatives.

> **DIANE:** (With her hand up like a traffic cop.) Stop! (After her boss has regained composure.) Your supervisor just gave you this report to do fifteen minutes ago. You've known for a long time that I have to go to the wedding rehearsal tonight and will be busy all day Saturday. I don't want to rush and do a poor job because that would make both of us look bad. I'd be happy to come in tonight after the rehearsal or on Sunday after the wedding to finish it. That way, you could get a quality report and I could keep my obligations. Is that okay?

Finally, remember that you cannot cure the difficult person. But you can manage the relationship so that you deal with them on an even, adult basis. (In Chapter 12 there will be many more examples of negotiations with various types of difficult people.)

As you can see from these examples, what makes negotiation work is not only the process, but understanding the people involved in the process.

Three Things Make Personality Negotiating Work

Personality Negotiating has three parts: 1) the way you communicate and negotiate; 2) the way the other side communicates and negotiates; and 3) the interactions between you and them. The first part of Personality Negotiating involves learning about your personal style. The second part is understanding others' styles. The third part is developing a strategy to make sure the mix of styles works well.

These three components of Personality Negotiating will be used throughout the book. You'll learn step-by-step techniques for adapting your approach in everyday, practical business situations.

Don't I Understand People Already?

Many negotiators understand the personality traits of the people they bargain with. They have learned through trial and error which strategies work with which types of people. If you are a seasoned negotiator and adapt your negotiating style to the various situations you deal with, Personality Negotiating will be a reinforcement that what you're doing is right and why your approach works. If you are an inexperienced negotiator, Personality Negotiating will help you avoid seat-of-the-pants learning. You'll know right away what can take others many years of trial-and-error-type negotiating to figure out.

How Personality Theory Helps in Negotiating

There are four ways in which the personality theory in Personality Negotiating can help in reaching agreements. They are by revealing:

1. **How communication flows most comfortably and effectively.**

   Craig just asked the members of his department if they have any questions or concerns about his proposal. After a good amount of time, they haven't said anything. Craig closes the meeting satisfied that everyone is happy. Should he be confident? (The answer is in chapter 3.)

2. **The type of information that sways people best.**

   Jenny is negotiating with her boss about her need for a budget increase. She has brought to the meeting thirty pages of neatly organized, impeccably accurate data that she believes proves her case. Will she be successful? (The answer is in chapter 4.)

3. **What convinces people to come to agreements.**

   Paul is negotiating a volume purchase agreement for computers. He's sure the secretaries will be happy with the computers because they'll save time and effort. Will they like the computers? (The answer is in chapter 5.)

4. **What perspective people have about time when they make a decision.**

   Boris wants the paper supplies contract wrapped up by Friday. He needs Cathy, his boss, to approve the purchase order to buy the supplies. Will he get the approval by Friday? (The answer is in chapter 6.)

We'll look at each of the above cases in detail in the coming chapters. What you'll find is that the answers to these, and other everyday situations, differ depending on whom you're dealing with. The tendency is to negotiate the way we would want others to negotiate with us. The problem is that this works only with those who think and act as we do.

Strategies that work well with one type of person, won't work with others. That's why you can't do cookie-cutter negotiations (negotiate the same way every time). With Personality Negotiating, you'll know how to, when to, and in what ways to deal with all types of people. That's why everyone will become an easy-to-negotiate-with person. It won't make any difference if they are good or bad negotiators at the start of the negotiation.

How to Deal with Poor Negotiators

If you're not dealing with good negotiators, you need to teach them negotiating skills. At the beginning of the American Revolution, General George Washington was faced with a militia made up of farmers to fight the British army. Since the farmers didn't know how to fight, he had to train them to be soldiers. As the saying goes, "If you have lemons, make lemonade."

Most of the time in any negotiation is spent educating the other side about your concerns and the negotiation process, and learning from them what their concerns are. Since negotiations go most smoothly when the parties involved are good negotiators, you'll learn specific, practical skills for training the other side in Personality Negotiating. If they don't know how to deal with you, you can teach them.

Personality Theory Is Proven in Business

Personality Negotiating uses personality theory to predict other people's behavior accurately. The personality theory in Personality Negotiating is based on Carl Jung's work on personality type.[1] Jungian personality type is measured in many ways, the two most common being the Kiersey and Bates temperament sorter and the Myers-Briggs Type Indicator (MBTI)®.[2] It's used in business today primarily as a management development tool. Two psychologists, Isabel Myers and Katherine Briggs, developed the MBTI to help people appreciate each other better. The MBTI has been used in business for over forty years and has been validated in hundreds of scientific studies. Thousands of companies, including Apple Computer, ITT, and Digital Equipment Corporation administered the MBTI and other Jungian personality-type measures over two million times last year.[3]

Many people, however, haven't heard of the MBTI, and they're unaware of its value in negotiations. Personality Negotiating, using the same Jungian concepts, describes and categorizes behavior four ways, with each category, or index, having two alternative preferences for a total of eight separate preferences.

The Eight Preferences

Here is a brief overview of the eight preferences and their individual relevance in negotiations. The preferences will be covered in detail and in combinations in the chapters ahead with examples of their usefulness in negotiations.

Index #1—Introvert/Extrovert

This first index, presented in chapter 3, is the Introvert/Extrovert index. It is useful when choosing how and where to communicate with people.

> **INTROVERT:** Introverts like to analyze information alone and consider questions before they speak.
> **IMPORTANCE TO NEGOTIATORS:** Make sure you send them information they need to understand your position before the negotiation. Also, when you ask them questions, wait for answers.

> **EXTROVERT:** Extroverts like to be in a group and enjoy discussing ideas.
> **IMPORTANCE TO NEGOTIATORS:** Meet with Extroverts regularly, and discuss ideas with them instead of giving them information to read.

Index #2—Sensing/Intuitive

The Sensing/Intuitive index (in chapter 4) is especially useful when you decide on the content of supporting data used in negotiations.

SENSING: Sensing types are convinced by data that is rich in facts, and they want answers to problems to have practical benefits; they'll notice every detail.
IMPORTANCE TO NEGOTIATORS: Give them what they want: fact, details, and practicality.

INTUITIVE: Intuitives need to know the theory behind an idea, and they don't want much detail.
IMPORTANCE TO NEGOTIATORS: Speak with them in terms of the big picture, and don't get bogged down in details.

Index #3—Thinking/Feeling

The Thinking/Feeling index (in chapter 5) comes into play when you're ironing out differences. It's what salespeople call handling objections. This index lets you know the type of objections to expect and the best way to deal with them.

THINKING: Thinking types make decisions objectively and analytically.
IMPORTANCE TO NEGOTIATORS: Stress the logical reasons for their accepting your bargaining points.

FEELING: Feeling types make decisions based on improving the quality of people's lives.
IMPORTANCE TO NEGOTIATORS: Stress the human benefits of coming to a decision.

Index #4—Judging/Perceiving

Finally, there is the Judging/Perceiving index (in chapter 6). The Judging/Perceiving index is the key indicator for knowing when to close a deal because it measures a person's view of time in decision making.

JUDGING: Judging types like making schedules and deadlines and keeping to them.
IMPORTANCE TO NEGOTIATORS: When you negotiate with Judging types, make sure you respect and keep to their schedules.

PERCEIVING: Perceiving types like flexible schedules and deadlines, and are careful decision makers.
IMPORTANCE TO NEGOTIATORS: Be flexible with the Perceiving types. They will be event driven, not time driven. Discovering the addressing key events that need to happen before they commit will drive the negotiation forward.

MBTI Shorthand

MBTI shorthand abbreviates each preference by its initial letter as follows:

Index 1	Index 2	Index 3	Index 4
E Extrovert	**S** Sensing	**T** Thinking	**J** Judging
I Introvert	**N** Intuitive	**F** Feeling	**P** Perceiving

Note: You can't use I for Intuitive in the second index because that letter is taken up by the Introvert preference in the first index.

According to MBTI theory, each of us leans towards one of the two preferences in each of the four Personality trait areas, or indexes. Our four index preferences, collectively, are our personality type. There are, therefore, sixteen possible personality types. (For example, one is the ESTJ, an Extroverted, Sensing, Thinking, Judging type.) No wonder people find others hard to figure out.

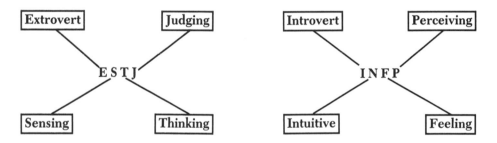

Most People Are Unaware of Their Preferences

Many of us are unaware we have the kind of preferences listed above, though we all do. For instance, Judging types tend to think of the perfect vacation as one that covers sixteen countries in twelve days, with every second planned and accounted for. Perceiving types might want to just get in their cars and start driving, taking each minute as it comes. While both ways are different, neither way is better. Making Judging types leave their watches and itineraries at home, or Perceiving types keep to a tight schedule is like making left-handers write with their right hands. They can do it, but it won't be natural, easy, or fun.

The Mechanics of Negotiation

Every negotiation is different. Yet, all types of negotiation share similar components and a general structure that will be looked at in chapter 2. Chapter 3 will begin the mingling of personality theory with negotiation skills.

Conclusion

Personality Negotiating makes impossible negotiations possible and possible negotiations easier. Personality Negotiating involves understanding your personal communication and negotiation styles and adapting them to the situation at hand. Many people feel the best part of Personality negotiating is that they can just be themselves. They don't have to say or do things that make them feel uncomfortable or silly. Personality Negotiating doesn't try to make you copy other successful negotiators, because what's right for one isn't right for all. Instead, Personality Negotiating gives you the tools to be the best version of who you are. The result is that everyone will walk away a winner.

What's Your Type?

To learn your personality type, answer the test questions in upcoming chapters or use the Negotiation Personality Guide at the back of this book. It isn't the Myers-Briggs Type Indicator, but it will give you a good idea of your preferences. The Negotiation Personality Guide is based on the answers that people who have taken the MBTI gave in Sales and Negotiation Training Company training seminars.

NOTES

1. Carl Jung, *Psychological Types* (New York: Harcourt Press, 1923).
2. The Myers-Briggs Type Indicator is a registered trademark of Consulting Psychologists Press, Inc., Palo Alto, California. The MBTI is a trademark of Consulting Psychologists Press, Inc., Palo Alto, California.
3. Thomas Moore, "Personality Tests Are Back," *Fortune* (March, 1987), 74–82.

Chapter 2
THE MECHANICS OF NEGOTIATION

You hear local news reports of on-going negotiations describe them as tough, hard-hitting, stalemated, laborious, tedious, or tense. The two sides negotiating, called adversaries, are said to be trying to weaken, coax, force, threaten, and to make demands of each other. This behavior goes on through the night, into the eleventh hour, with no hope in sight, and so on, until one side caves in, crashes, submits, or is forced into a deal.

Many of us think that negotiating is like the process just described. But what was described is battling, not negotiating.

Constructive negotiations are, admittedly, less sensational. Can you imagine the following live mini-cam report:

> **NEWS REPORTER:** The two parties in the negotiation have a clear understanding of each other's needs. They are developing a collaborative solution to the issues that will benefit everyone.

That report lacks the drama and tension that people think "must" happen during negotiations. Having an understanding of others' needs and developing collaborative solutions is what negotiation is actually all about, not animosity. Negotiation courses disappoint some students because they want to learn how to battle those that are battling them. "Understanding needs? Collaborative solutions? With that jerk? You're crazy!" is a common first response to effective negotiation skills.

"That Jerk" Might Have a Point

Usually, "that jerk" is someone who has needs and concerns that aren't appreciated. And maybe they aren't very understanding of your perspective either. Personality Negotiating works because both parties benefit. A rule of thumb is that battling is always available as an option, so use it only as a last resort. Those who use battling as a trump card find that they don't need to use it very often.

Before getting into specific strategies that you can tailor to your personality, let's look at the concepts common to all negotiations. First, we'll spend a little more time on what negotiation is.

What Negotiation Is

Negotiation is the process by which two or more parties come to a mutually beneficial agreement. Each party has something the other party wants and, in return, can give something the other party needs. During the negotiation, each party gives what they can to get what they need. All negotiations share one goal: having both parties come out better than when they started. Negotiation is a process because there are several steps to the successful conclusion of a negotiation. During the negotiation process, both parties explain to each other what they can offer the other side, what they need from the other side, and the reasons why both parties will come out ahead when they agree on a deal.

You may not realize it, but you negotiate many times each day. Not all negotiations are long and complex. When you stop using the copy machine for a minute, so that someone else can be ready for a meeting, that's a negotiation. This chapter will look at those steps in detail.

There are many types of negotiations that take place in business. The negotiation techniques and the process of explaining needs, desires, and reasons to negotiate are the same for all types of negotiations. There are three essential ingredients to a successful negotiation: 1) parties willing to negotiate; 2) sincere questioning of each other to discover needs; and 3) a desire to maintain a relationship.

Wanting the Other Side to Succeed

The first ingredient in a successful negotiation is the desire of the parties involved to want or need the other person or group in the negotiation to succeed. The following is *not* a negotiation:

> The United Union Workers are upset that the Northeast Steel Company is experiencing 50 percent profits each year, while they get a 5 percent raise. They enter the negotiations wanting to get every cent they can from Northeast. They don't care if the strike goes on so long that Northeast goes out of business.
>
> Northeast Steel doesn't like being unionized and wishes the workers will go on strike so they can hire non-union labor. The management thinks the union is unreasonable and whining. They are confident a strike won't hurt their business and welcome such an action.

If you ask most people what negotiation is, they'll tell you the antitheses of negotiation and, instead, give you the definition of debating or battling: "Getting as much as you can by giving as little as you have to."

Unfortunately, when parties battle they generally lose. Even the winners get less on the battlefield than they would have at the negotiation table. And, in a war, even in one-sided victories lives are lost on both sides. "Wars of attrition" and Eastern Airlines vs. the mechanic's union are both examples of battles with no winners, only losers.

A year after the United Union Workers went on strike, Northeast went out of business. Since the stockholders saw the negative effects of a long-term strike months in advance, they sold their shares. This left Northeast unable to buy raw materials and necessary capital equipment.

Because foreign competitors took Northeast's contracts, no one bought the mill, so the workers became unemployed and had to move to other parts of the country to get jobs.

The result of the battle was both parties losing.

Good negotiation isn't "getting" concessions while "giving up" little. Negotiation isn't debating or battling because, rather than having a winner and a loser, good negotiations have two winners.

The Standard of Fairness

A deal is fair when you can honestly say that both parties are coming out equally well and that, given the choice, you would take either side. For instance:

Bob had his house listed for $140,000 and Donna originally offered him $120,000 for it. They negotiated a price of $135,000.

The deal would be fair if: 1) Bob would buy a house similar to his for $135,000 and, 2) If Donna were selling the house she bought, she'd take $135,000 for it. If Bob wouldn't buy the house or Donna wouldn't sell because they thought the deal wasn't fair, then it isn't fair.

Concerns vs. Positions

To make sure that everyone wins, the negotiators need to explain the concerns that are important to them. The key to understanding is listening and information gathering. "Things that are important to them" can be either concerns or stated as positions. Let's look at what concerns and positions are and how they are different.

Positions

Positions are opinions and feelings about people, places, things, ideas, or anything else. One must accept another's opinions as the way he feels and not try to change his convictions. You can't negotiate opinions because diverse opinions are equally valid. You can never convince people that their opinions are wrong, because they never are. Take, for instance, a woman who thinks that skiing in the mountains is the ideal vacation. Her husband's opinion is that going to the tropics is the best vacation. Both feel that their opinions, or positions, on the optimal vacation are correct, and both are one hundred percent right. She likes the mountains. He likes swimming. They could argue all day (as some couples do before a vacation) about the best choice with no resolution because both are completely right. She's one hundred percent right that she feels skiing is better, and he's one hundred percent right that he feels the beach is better. After people state their position, there's nothing to do but accept the stated opinion and move on.

Concerns

Concerns are different from positions. Concerns can be discussed and adapted, unlike opinions, which must be accepted for what they are. Concerns are the *reasons* for what people want, not what they say they want. One can usually satisfy concerns in many ways. For example, George is a self-employed accountant who wants to spend less time working. His goal, or concern, is to have more free time while still keeping up with his client base. He believes that the best way to reach his goal is to find a partner. (His position is that he needs a partner.) George is not altogether happy with this solution, however, because it will take several months for a partner to generate enough new business to justify his or her income. To discover an optimal solution, George needs to remake the connection between positions and concerns and rethink them.

Finding What You "Really" Need

Step 1: Remake the Connection Between Positions and Concerns

The first thing George needs to do is to list ways that could possibly give him more free time:

Get a partner — w/cust. base
Buy a computer
Take time off
Hire a Temp
Take work on vacation

Step 2: Examine the Pros and Cons of Each Alternative

OPTION A: Get a partner

Two busy accountants will still have no free time, but the practice will grow.

OPTION B: Buy a computer

A computer will take awhile to learn, but will eventually handle faster much of the clerical work now done by hand.

OPTION C: Take time off

It took too long to develop the client base to risk losing them now.

OPTION D: Hire a temp

A temporary accountant would handle the peak loads, but could pirate customers.

A temporary bookkeeper could handle the peak loads, and would be inexpensive.

OPTION E: Take work on vacation

Yuk!

What George is doing by creating these lists is analyzing the alternative solutions apart from his wanting to have a partner.

Step 3: Select the Best Choice Based on the Reasons Given

Although he originally wanted a partner, George needed to analyze the reasons for that choice with the same scrutiny as the other choices he listed. Negotiators call this "separating the person from the problem."

George now reasons that a computer would take care of most of his time-consuming clerical work quickly, and could even be used to submit tax returns for his clients. Though a computer would take time to learn, long term he'd save many hours.

Separating the Person from the Problem

Roger Fisher in *Getting to Yes* says to "separate the person from the problem."[1] This means negotiators should focus on the problem, instead of the negotiators' opinions about the problem. Doing that makes the parties focus on concerns and makes negotiation easier, and often makes it possible. When people get emotionally involved in an argument, it makes it difficult for them to see beyond their strongly held positions. Here are some examples of concerns and positions:

Position	Concern
Your prices are too high	I need a pine fence, not the more expensive redwood one.
If I can't buy today, I'll assume you don't want to do business with me.	I need to hear from your bank to complete the credit application. They haven't called me back yet.
Your company hasn't been in business long enough.	I want to deal with engineers who are experienced, because my project is complex.
You're driving too fast.	You wouldn't have time to stop in case of an emergency.

As you can see from the position column, each statement can be responded to with a counterposition. "You're driving too fast," will be met with, "No, I'm not." One person absolutely feels another is going too fast, while the other absolutely feels that's not the case. They can argue forever and never come to a resolution. Why? Again, because both are one hundred percent right in their positions.

Here's an example with Rebecca, the skier, and her husband, Steve, the swimmer. They're planning a vacation for January as they are both in need of a break:

Rebecca's goals: 1) To have a vacation in which she can have fun. 2) To pick a location that Steve will like, too. 3) To get skiing in before the end of the winter.

Steve's goals: 1) To have a vacation in which he can have fun. 2) To pick a location Rebecca will like, too. 3) To get away from the cold and into the warm sunshine.

Step 1: Assert Positions

> **REBECCA:** I want to go on a skiing vacation. (Rebecca's position is that she wants to ski.)
> **STEVE:** I want to go someplace warm. (Steve's position is that they should go south.)

Step 2: Define Terms

> **REBECCA:** What do you mean by "warm"? (Information query.)
> **STEVE:** I mean where you can swim. (Steve's idea of swimming is outside.)
> **REBECCA:** Okay (acceptance of a fact), there are pools at ski lodges, and you could use one of them. (This is a trial balloon. Rebecca wants to see how Steve feels about her suggestion.)
> **STEVE:** I want to get a tan on a beach, not in a tanning booth. (Steve gives Rebecca more information to clarify his position.) Why do you want to go skiiing?
> **REBECCA:** Because I like the air rushing by when I'm going fast on skis. (Rebecca states her position.)
> **STEVE:** Why don't you go water skiing? (Steve suggests an alternative.)
> **REBECCA:** It's not the same. I want to be in control, coming down a mountainside, not dragged behind a boat. (Rebecca states her position.)

Now that they have each asserted their concerns, it's time for the next step.

Step 3: Explore Alternatives

> **REBECCA:** I don't need to ski every day, and I want to ski with you, not alone. I like your idea about going to the ocean, but with lift lines so long on weekends, I just don't feel like skiing then. This vacation is the only chance I'll have to go mid-week. (Rebecca begins collaborative problem solving.)
> **STEVE:** I like skiing with you, I just don't want to ski for a week in the cold, and flying to a warm place just for a weekend isn't worth the money.

Step 4: Discover the Real Concern

The real goal is finding a place where they can go together: where there is a mountain for skiing (for Rebecca), and a beach warm enough to swim (for Steve).

> **REBECCA:** Why don't we go to California? The mountains are only about an hour from the beach. There, we could ski or swim part of the day or on certain days and do the other the rest of the time.
>
> **STEVE:** Great idea! Let's make reservations.

Steve and Rebecca could have argued for hours on whose vacation idea was better. The arguments would have been fruitless, since the real concern was finding a place that was right for both of them. When the place was discovered as the concern, Rebecca's wanting to ski, or Steve's wanting to swim was replaced by a discussion of what should be done apart from how they felt. They separated the person from the problem.

When parties start arguing without a resolution, or when a negotiation breaks down into the parties repeating their opinions, it's a stalemate. Fortunately, stalemates can be broken.

Breaking Stalemates

Stalemates happen for many reasons. Usually they happen because one or both parties don't have the motivation to negotiate, or don't know how to deal with each other. The first way to avoid a stalemate is to negotiate at the proper time.

Stalemate #1: Optimal Timing in Negotiations

If one party isn't ready to negotiate, little can be done in a negotiation. When someone doesn't want to bargain, the other could offer anything and it wouldn't be accepted. Stalemates also happen when one party wants something the other party has, but cannot offer anything in return. For example, Linda wants to lease a parcel of land to open an office supply store. The owner, Cindy, is happy with the land's being vacant and does not care if it's unimproved.

Your strategy must be to motivate the other side by showing them the advantages of coming to a deal.

> **LINDA:** I will offer you a ten-year lease. During that time, instead of having to pay taxes on a vacant lot, you'll be making money.

CINDY: Taxes on the land aren't that steep, and I wouldn't make enough on the lease to justify holding up the property.
LINDA: What if you became a silent partner? I would give you fifteen percent of the profits in return for the use of a larger share of land. This way, I could spend money on a bigger store, I wouldn't have to worry about losing my lease, and you would get a larger return on the land than from renting it.
CINDY: I like that idea. Let's look into it more.

If you are in negotiations with an unmotivated party, don't give up. If you can't deal with one person, you are likely to find others who want to deal with you.

Don't Leave Things on a Sour Note

If the timing isn't right, don't burn your bridges. You may have to deal with that person again.

"Sorry we couldn't come to a deal. We'll talk later when the circumstances are better."

Another way negotiations get stalemated is that they are proceeding with the wrong party.

Stalemate #2: Negotiating with the Wrong People

The second reason negotiations get stalled is that they are taking place with participants who don't have the authority to reach a decision.

Your strategy is to ask if the party you're dealing with is the decision maker. If that person is not the decision maker, ask to get the individual in charge involved.

Ramone is looking to put an addition onto his house. He needs to get the approval of the town. He has been speaking with Jerry, the town engineer, who is not being supportive. Jerry does not have the authority to sign the building permit. His boss, Helen, does.

RAMONE: I'm going to invite Helen to our next meeting. That way we can get feedback from all involved in the decision making process.

When going over someone's head, be careful not to step on their toes while you are doing it. If you explain that you are interested in involving the decision maker, too, then no one's feelings should be hurt.

The next reason there's reluctance to "pull the trigger" is that some will worry that they are not getting a fair deal.

Stalemate #3: Have I Given Away Too Much?

One reason people are reluctant to negotiate is that they feel they could be giving away more than needed to get an agreement. It's impossible to precisely measure when you've given away an excessive amount. Often, this is because the more you give, the more you'll get back. If the deal is fair and you both come out winners, then you didn't give away the farm.

One strategy many fearful negotiators use is to bring ridiculously low offers to the table and increase the offers in small increments. (They operate according to the myth that one's first offer should never be accepted. The theory is that, if the offer is accepted, you could have gotten by with offering less, and you don't know how much less that would have been.) Bill uses this strategy when buying a house:

> "I'll offer you one hundred dollars for your three bedroom, two-bath house with seven acres of land. . . . How about two hundred? . . ."

Bill's first offer is, of course, not accepted, but the seller of the house now marks him as an insincere, or insecure, negotiator. The seller refuses even to talk with Bill after his offer reaches eight hundred dollars. If your first offer is a fair offer that will have you both come out winners, be pleased, not disappointed, if it is taken:

> **BILL:** I know you're asking a hundred and twenty thousand for your home, but there is a similar home across town for one hundred thousand. Since your home has a garage, I'll offer you one hundred and five.
> **SELLER:** I'll take it.

Bill got the house he wanted at the price he wanted. He should be happy.

It's not difficult to measure your breaking point, or when a deal doesn't make sense to commit to. This is what Fisher and Ury call your Best Alternative to a Negotiated Agreement, or BATNA.[2]

Know Your BATNA

The Best Alternative to a Negotiated Agreement is, generally speaking, the outcome if no negotiations take place. That is, what would happen if you halt the negotiations and reach no agreement at all.

Assuming you should be negotiating, you need to figure out when would be the proper time to give up. For that, you need to know your bottom line. Your bottom line is the crossover point into a losing deal for you, or when you'd be worse off, not better off, with an agreement.

Assessing your BATNA and your bottom line before the negotiation is very important. Before the negotiation, you can think with a cool head, and can look at a situation in a somewhat detached fashion. If, all of a sudden, you start to get pressured during a negotiation, you might make an agreement that you'll later regret—one that's below your bottom line.

Knowing your BATNA has positive effects, too. You'll always know your agreement is a good one. The next reason negotiations stalemate is the opposite of thinking that you've been too generous—worrying that you haven't gotten enough.

Stalemate #4: Could I Be Getting More?

Again, a lot of us worry that we're not getting enough. This goes back to the fallacy that negotiating is giving up as little as you can to get as much as you can. This description is wrong because if you take advantage of someone in a negotiation, they won't want to deal with you anymore. Still, you want to get a fair deal. You do this by knowing the other side's BATNA, as well as your own.

Know the Other Side's BATNA

Next, spend some time thinking about the other side's BATNA. Since they're negotiating with you, you know that they want to gain something. Knowing their BATNA will give you an idea of when you are asking for too many concessions.

> Lisa is negotiating an employment contract during an economy with high unemployment. The employer's BATNA is hiring one of several other qualified applicants.
>
> It is proper for Lisa to seek a win–win deal, but if she asks for too much, it could harm the negotiation.
>
> Here, Lisa should ask for standard concessions, but not expect that she get four weeks vacation if the norm is two weeks.

Knowing the other side's BATNA also gives you a sense of what you need to give up to make a deal.

> Jill's prospective employer wants her to work seventy-five hours a week. Jill knows that no one in her field would work that many hours for the salary offered. She knows she does not

have to give that concession to get the job because her prospective employer's BATNA is hiring no one.

Thinking about the BATNA of the people you're negotiating with is time well spent. This will make things easier if the going gets tough.

A good way to learn about the folks you're negotiating with is to have a meeting before the formal negotiation begins. This will prevent surprises that can sometimes creep up during the meeting. More on this topic in chapter 4.

Conclusion

Negotiation is giving what you can to get what you need. When you negotiate, make sure you want the other side to succeed and listen to the concerns. Concerns are ultimate wants or desires, and can be negotiated while opinions must only be accepted. Finally, when negotiating, separate the people from the problem and know your BATNA—Best Alternative to a Negotiated Agreement.

NOTES

1. Roger Fisher and William Ury, *Getting to Yes: Negotiating Agreements Without Giving In* (New York: Houghton Mifflin, 1981), 101.
2. Fisher and Ury, *Getting to Yes*, 101.

Chapter 3
OPENING UP COMMUNICATION LINES

Again and again you hear that communication is important in negotiations. It's true. Negotiations couldn't happen without it. Collaborative solutions begin and end with each party knowing what the other party wants. Linguists tell us that command of language is instinctual, and that everybody can understand and be understood by others. Linguists also tell us that eighty to ninety percent of what we hear is not based on the words, but on our assumption of what the words said.

That's why the party game "telephone" works. That's the game in which players pass a message along, each repeating what they thought they heard to the next person. When a piece of the message is missed or forgotten, it's filled in with assumptions. After a while the message gets so garbled that what the last person in the chain hears frequently bears no resemblance to what the first person said.

The Orange-Juice Dilemma

Technically, the telephone game works because many sounds that we "hear" aren't sounds at all, but vibrations our ear translates into sounds for our brain to register. For instance, the J sound in orange and juice is one sound that we "hear" that doesn't show up on a spectrograph.

If someone says, "Will you please pass the orange juice?" you think that you hear the sentence. What you actually hear is, "ill u please pass e orge uice?" Your brain fills in the rest.

The Orange-Juice Dilemma in Negotiations

The orange-juice dilemma cripples many negotiations. Someone is confident his thoughts have been communicated and understood. Someone else is confident that he understood the message. In reality, neither event happened.

By anticipating what others say, many times people "understand" something far different from what was intended to be communicated. According to management writer Peter Drucker, in a controlled study, excellent speakers presented information to excellent listeners for ten minutes. Each knew that the listeners would be questioned on the material immediately following the presentation. The highest comprehension level was twenty-five percent.

Listening Between the Lines

Nature and language give us hurdles to cross. Besides the dynamics of speech, everyone has a unique style of interaction, according to his or her personality type. This is related to the first area of Personality Negotiating, the Introvert/Extrovert preference. We'll look at that next.

Although we are all diverse, we share certain traits that we, and others, can key in on. This is useful in negotiation because lines of communication can be opened with less effort for everyone when you and the people you're negotiating with match styles.

Step 1: Open Up the Communication Lines Using Personality Type

The best way to open the lines of communication is to focus your efforts on dealing with people the way they want to be dealt with. To exemplify this, we'll look at the first area of Personality Negotiating—the Introvert/ Extrovert preference. This preference determines: 1) when we like to meet; 2) one way we want information presented to us; 3) our thinking process; and 4) our verbal communication pattern.

The Introvert/Extrovert Index

The first of the four areas of Personality Negotiating is the Introvert/ Extrovert index. This index shows how we prefer to interact with others. The kinds of interaction that are critical to successful negotiations are meeting times and types, and conversation patterns. As you'll see, Introverts and Extroverts want contacts, meetings, and the flow of conversation managed in completely opposite ways. Choosing the correct method makes the negotiation easier, and often makes it possible, because the wrong type of contact will be met with little if any enthusiasm.

Introverts and Extroverts find being alone a very different experience. Introverts do their most productive thinking when alone. They're energized when they're in their offices with the door closed. Extroverts, on the other hand, do their finest thinking in forums where they can share and develop ideas with others. Extroverts find lunchroom get-togethers or a large meeting energizing. They find being alone draining.

In business, there is about a fifty-fifty split of Introverts and Extroverts. Still, certain occupations tend to attract one type over the other. For instance, bookkeepers and managers tend to be Introverts, and salespeople tend to be Extroverts.[1] While both Introverts and Extroverts can be excellent negotiators, they have profoundly diverse styles. Which type are you? If you're interested, answer the following questions.

DIRECTIONS: Read each of these ten items and circle answer A or B, depending on which fits you best. There are no right, wrong, or better answers. You'll find the key to scoring at the end of the test.

1. **If someone asks you a question, you usually:**
   A) reflect for a few moments, then respond.
   B) respond immediately.
2. **You like:**
   A) short meetings.
   B) long meetings.
3. **You would rather go out with a few friends:**
   A) to a crowded party.
   B) to a quiet restaurant.
4. **When someone wants you to get back to them with information, you prefer:**
   A) writing them a proposal and sending it to them.
   B) meeting with them and talking about it.
5. **You prefer being with people who are:**
   A) somewhat talkative.
   B) very talkative.
6. **You would rather have:**
   A) a desk in an open area.
   B) a desk off by itself.
7. **You find your most tiring days to be:**
   A) days when you meet many new people.
   B) days when you are alone.
8. **If there is a long period of silence during a conversation, it is your inclination to:**
   A) fill it in.
   B) use it to think.
9. **You prefer:**
   A) having someone introduce you.
   B) introducing yourself to someone.
10. **If a phone call has to be made, you would prefer**
    A) having someone else make it.
    B) making it yourself.

11. When you leave a room after a spirited discussion, you are more likely to think:
A) why did I say that?
B) why didn't I say something?

SCORING:
Add the **A** answers for questions
1, 2, 4, 5, 7, 9, 10
Add the **B** answers for questions
3, 6, 8, 11

Put the Total here:_____ **I/E**

If the Total is 6 or more, you're most likely an **Introvert**. Otherwise, you're most likely an **Extrovert**. (NOTE: Although this is not the Myers-Briggs Type Indicator®, it will give you an idea of what your type is, as it is based on answers people have given who have taken the MBTI.)

Occupations Common to Introverts and Extroverts

Following are lists of occupations that have a predominance of Introverts and Extroverts.[2] While one type may predominate in a field, there's always a mix of both types. (Every salesperson isn't an Extrovert, every banker isn't an Introvert.)

Introverts Predominate	Extroverts Predominate
manager	salesperson
banker	marketer
engineer	police officer
accountant	construction worker
farmer	receptionist
mechanic	waiter/waitress
programmer	teacher
surveyor	nurse
psychiatrist	office manager
social worker	cleric
researcher	lawyer
photographer	politician

As you can see from the lists, Introverts prefer occupations and professions that allow them to be alone and think things out themselves.

They prefer a moderate to low amount of human interaction. Extroverts prefer professions that allow them to talk with others regularly and frequently, which is why so many Extroverts are in the sales and marketing fields.

When to Open Negotiations

Before you begin the negotiations, set up the forum that is best for everyone with whom you are trying to strike a deal. Most people, as teenagers, learned through trial and error when and where to negotiate with their parents for privileges or the use of the family car. They could try: 1) when their parents first get home from work; 2) during dinner; or 3) an hour after dinner. If their parents are Introverts, they know to wait until after dinner. If their parents are Extroverts, they know their best chance is to broach the subject when their parents just get home, or during dinnertime conversation.

Personality Negotiating Eliminates Trial and Error

Introverts and Extroverts are predictable in their preferred time and place for negotiations. Choosing the proper atmosphere will make the negotiations flow smoothly, while choosing the wrong atmosphere will make the negotiation difficult for everyone.

Negotiating with Introverts

The optimal time to meet with Introverts is after they've had a chance to be by themselves awhile. This is because human contact and conversation tend to be exhausting for the Introvert. You'll have better luck negotiating with Introverts when they're fresh and alert. Although people's preferences differ, the best times to meet with an Introvert are the first thing in the morning, around lunch time, or at the end of the day. The conversations should be short and there should be few people present. When practical, one-to-one negotiations are best. Introverts prefer scheduled meetings over impromptu ones. At the meeting, Introverts will want to get down to business quickly without engaging in extended chitchat beforehand.

Negotiating with Extroverts

Anytime will be good for Extroverts to discuss an issue with you because they enjoy conferences and discussions. Large meetings tend to be better for Extroverts. They'll usually want to talk for a while about non-business-related subjects; especially if they've been alone in the office for a good chunk of time beforehand. Being alone is tiring to Extroverts. They need social interaction to "charge their batteries"[3] before they can start talking turkey.

How to Discover a Person's Type

You can find out others' Introvert/Extrovert preference by listening and observing. No one's purely an Introvert or Extrovert, but everyone has a preference. A person's preference is his or her most comfortable way of dealing with others, and what thought processes the person finds most suitable, if given a choice. There are times when Extroverts choose to be alone and when Introverts choose to discuss a problem with several friends.

Jungian psychologists say that everyone has a single preference within each index, or area, of personality testing. You discover others' Introvert/Extrovert preference by asking these types of questions:

> "I have a solution to the problem we were discussing. We could talk about it now, or I could send you a report, and you could get back to me. Which would you prefer?"

Extroverts will want to discuss the solution. Introverts will prefer to see the report and reflect on it first.

> "Would you prefer I call you with the answer or fax it to you?"

Extroverts will prefer the call. Introverts will prefer the fax.

Asking and Answering Questions

Introverts and Extroverts think over and respond to questions very differently because their thought processes are not alike. Extroverts like to verbalize what they're thinking, while Introverts prefer thinking to themselves for about ten seconds before they speak. This difference leads to misunderstandings that can hamper negotiations.

Questions To and From Extroverts

Extroverts tend to rely on talking much more than Introverts do. When negotiating with Extroverts, you'll need to converse extensively to bring the negotiation to a successful conclusion.

BEHAVIOR: Extroverts will answer questions immediately and verbalize what they're thinking. They want to talk about solutions instead of studying them privately.

THINGS TO WATCH OUT FOR: Hearing all their thoughts means you'll hear contradictory or premature ideas. Be careful not to interpret developing ideas as conclusions.

For example, you just asked Glenn, an Extrovert, which of three cities he thinks should be the location of the new sales office. He immediately says:

> "Well, Boston is the biggest city with the largest market. Hartford has the biggest growth potential. Nashua, New Hampshire, seems the most cost-effective choice."

Extroverts will start speaking almost immediately and tell you exactly what they're thinking. Negotiating with Extroverts is easier in some ways than negotiating with Introverts, but more difficult in other ways. When Extroverts verbalize their thoughts, they're doing you a favor by letting you know what they're thinking. On the other hand, what they say is not always what they mean. In the example above, Glenn speaks positively about all three cities. Still, you don't know for sure which city is his choice for the new office, if any. Therein lies the problem. Glenn says Boston is the biggest, Hartford has the most potential, and Nashua is the most cost-effective. It sounds to you as if Nashua is the winner, since he mentions it last, but it could actually be that he's interested in Hartford, the city with the biggest growth potential. It just isn't obvious from what he says, since each Extroverted statement sounds like a "conclusion." So, after Extroverts tell you their options, ask another question: "What is your decision?"

> "I think I'll recommend Hartford because the insurance industry is an untapped market for our products."

Questions To and From Introverts

Introverts tend to rely on their ability to process information in their heads, and rely less on their verbal skills. When negotiating with Introverts, place more importance on thinking about solutions, and spend less time talking and arguing.

BEHAVIOR: Introverts will prefer to reflect on questions silently. They'll reflect for about ten seconds before speaking.

THINGS TO WATCH OUT FOR: Interrupting Introverts while they think halts their internal deliberations. Large groups tend to be devitalizing, and often overwhelming to them. Introverts don't express themselves best in this environment. For example, when you ask Mark, an Introvert, about his choice of city, he thinks to himself for about fifteen seconds, then says,

"I'd say we locate the office in Hartford."

Mark's Introverted deliberating procedure is not the same as Glenn's Extroverted one. Instead of vocalizing alternatives, as Glenn did, Mark debates internally and only announces the conclusion.

The Extroverted Glenn began speaking almost immediately, while Mark waited fifteen seconds before speaking. Introverts need time to formulate responses to questions. *If you don't allow them that time to reflect, you won't get answers.*

Introverts are doing you a favor by giving you their conclusions, but sometimes they won't express how they reached their conclusion unless they are asked. If you feel you need the rationale behind an Introverted statement, ask for clarification: "How did you come to that conclusion?"

The Ineffective Way to Question Introverts

Greg, an Extrovert, tries to negotiate the support of Introverted Mark:

"Mark, after reviewing our data supporting Boston as the choice of the new sales office, do you have any questions?"

After waiting a few seconds for Mark to respond, and thinking that his reasons for choosing Boston were so clear no questions would be possible, Greg continues:

"I think Boston is the number one choice. Can I count on your support when we send this up to management for approval?"

Unknowingly, Greg has cut Mark off in mid-thought. Mark starts to respond:

"All right, b—"

Greg jumps in and gives himself the nod:

"Great. I'll let you know how it turns out."

Greg leaves the negotiation confident that he has Mark's full support, which he doesn't. Greg first missed key input by cutting Mark off in mid-thought. The second time, by interrupting his response, Greg missed his last opportunity to get Mark's true reaction.

The Effective Way to Question Introverts

Here's the effective way to sell to Introverts like Mark.

"Are there any questions?"

Wait. Don't assume there aren't any questions. Waiting is difficult for Extroverts, so if you are one, count to ten slowly to yourself.
After thinking to himself, Mark says:

"I know Boston is a large market, but I'm concerned that there is too much competition."

Because you heard the concern, you can address it:

"Where do you think would be better?"
"Hartford, because it has a large base of insurance companies and is growing economically. We would have a better chance there of securing a significant market share."
"You're right. Let's recommend Hartford."

Any time you negotiate with Introverts, let them speak without interruption. When you're dealing with Extroverts, make sure you know exactly which of the Extrovert's statements are conclusions and which are developing thoughts.

General Personality Negotiating with Introverts and Extroverts

When Personality Negotiating, remember that Extroverts enjoy discussions and frequent and large meetings, and will speak as they think.

Introverts opt to review documents by themselves and get the most out of small, infrequent meetings. They spend time thinking about what they say and verbalize only their conclusion.

To make your negotiations easy and successful, take charge and make sure the discussions happen at the appropriate time. Like the teenager asking for the car, you'll have much more success when the environment and the timing of questions is optimal.

Throughout the rest of the book there will be examples of ways to apply what you've learned about Introverts and Extroverts to a variety of negotiating situations.

Step 2: Make Sure You Get Everyone Involved

In groups, there are usually some individuals who speak out a lot, others who speak very little, and some, not at all. This is a prescription for disaster in a negotiation. Solutions negotiated without addressing the concerns of each member of the group will not get the support from all members of the group.

> A common negotiating exercise consists of two parts. The first part is to have several participants negotiate a single group decision. After the group returns, the second part begins. The participants each rate their feelings about the negotiation experience by writing on a piece of paper, on a scale of from one to ten, two things: 1) how the decision reflects their feelings on the subject and, 2) how much they are going to support the group in the implementation of the plan. They also note how much involvement they had during the negotiation.
>
> The participants who contributed their thoughts during the negotiation rate both categories high, usually eight or higher. This is true even if the final solution was different from the solution they endorsed.
>
> Those who didn't participate in the negotiation rate both categories low, usually four or lower. This is true even when the solution was similar to the one they endorsed.

After a deal fails, those who dominated the meeting throw up their hands and say, "We got input from everyone concerned."

The silent members of the groups throw up their hands and say, "No one asked us what we thought, so we assumed they didn't care."

If everyone puts their hands down and begins Personality Negotiating, they'll have much more success.

Ask Introverts for Their Opinions

Introverts assume that if you don't ask them for their opinions, you're not interested. Extroverts assume that if you don't say anything, it's because you don't have anything to say. Both assumptions are dead wrong.

Introverts report that their biggest cause of frustration in a negotiation is that no one cares what they think. Introverts frequently have a lot to say. Since Introverts have been listening and internally debating what is being said by both sides during the negotiation, more times than not they are like a gold mine waiting to be discovered.

Experience proves this time and time again by going around the table and asking each Introvert individually if they have anything to offer. If they get time to think and to speak, you usually won't be treated to silence, but to well thought out, useful comments.

Have Extroverts Stop and Think

Extroverts tend to be thinking about what they're going to say next as the person they are talking with is speaking. When it's their turn to speak (or they've interrupted) they will continue thinking about what they want to say, but verbalize their thoughts. If an Extrovert agrees with a point, he is likely to acknowledge that point to himself and move on with his thoughts.

This can sometimes cause the other party to feel that they are not being listened to. That is an understandable perception, but an inaccurate conclusion.

Extroverts need to verbally acknowledge others' points, so others know the Extroverts are listening. No one likes to be, or feel, ignored.

> **DIANE:** Flextime during the summer hours would increase job satisfaction by allowing the employees more recreational time.
>
> **BRAD:** Arranging meetings would be difficult. Starting times, leaving times, and lunches would be too staggered.

Brad's response is ineffective because, between the lines, Diane hears the following message:

> "Meetings are more important than recreation. Your idea is stupid, unworkable, and not worth considering."

Look at the difference here:

> **BRAD (EFFECTIVE RESPONSE):** Flextime is a good idea that I think we should consider seriously. My concerns are that with all the varied schedules, getting together for meetings will be difficult.

This response is effective, because Diane hears:

> "You have a good idea. I have some valid concerns and I want to solve a mutual problem."

Negotiation takes place.

DIANE: Your concerns about meeting times are good ones. What if we institute a core time, say from 10:00 until 3:00, when everyone has to be available. That way meetings can take place during those hours and schedules can still be flexible.

BRAD: Good solution. Let's do it.

What Did You Say?

A technique used in couples counselling is effective in negotiations. The idea is that one doesn't respond to a concern until he or she can suitably rephrase and repeat that concern back to his or her partner. The rule is that a partner must restate in his or her own words what the other means.

Not surprisingly, especially with deep-seated concerns, it takes a few tries to convince the other side you understand their position.

Step 3: Show Them Their Positions Have Merit

People want to feel that their ideas and values have merit. We not only appreciate having our ideas understood, we feel good about the folks we talk to when they react positively to us while they listen. We tend to like people who listen to us and to dislike those who don't.

When we are the listeners, rewarding others by showing them that we enjoy listening to them is easy if we really do agree with them. Preaching to the converted, or saying things that we know will be agreed with, is easy because we have a captive audience.

Often in negotiations, you don't have that luxury. Let's face it, negotiations aren't always a love-in where everybody is telling everybody else how wonderful they are. Labor negotiations, divorce negotiations, and pre-war negotiations are punctuated by deep-seated hostility. For these, and other negotiations, an appreciation of, not agreement with, another's views is what needs to happen.

Appreciation Is Not the Same as Agreement

To have a successful negotiation it is never necessary to agree with the other side. You must, however, appreciate their position. Here are examples of the reactions to appreciative and non-appreciative negotiators.

APPRECIATIVE NEGOTIATOR: I understand what you're saying, and you make a very good case for your issues. Though I agree with you on some points, I disagree with you on other points because I see the data as pointing to another conclusion.

REACTION: I'm glad you listened to me, though you have a different conclusion. Now I'm going to listen to you, too.

NON-APPRECIATIVE NEGOTIATOR: The answer is there in black and white. Only an idiot couldn't see that.

REACTION: If you weren't such a pompous jerk, maybe I'd listen to you.

When people feel others don't appreciate the merit in what they're saying, the usual outcomes are 1) attacking and escalating the animosity, or 2) avoiding the aggressor and halting the negotiation.

If you agree with a position, fine. If you're the type of person that finds it easy to appreciate another's position, that will make negotiation easier. If you're having trouble understanding a viewpoint that is contrary to yours, or "where they're coming from," just ask and emphasize.

Asking and emphasizing tells others that you don't understand them, but want to understand. All but the most difficult of people will work as hard at explaining as you are at listening. The longer the process goes on, the narrower the negotiation gaps become.

Ask and Empathize

Understanding is like a buried treasure. Sometimes you'll have to search, and dig, and probe, and sweat. But you'll get there, eventually. One technique, popularized by psychologist Carl Rogers, is reflecting back the feelings of the person you're negotiating with. If it's done sincerely, it can be very effective. Here's how it works:

CHRIS: I hate my commute. It takes two hours to get to work, and I feel that I work four hours a day without getting paid.
JOHN: You feel frustrated.
CHRIS: Of course I do. I wish there was a solution.
JOHN: I wonder what you could do?
CHRIS: Maybe I could take a class and study on the train.
JOHN: Maybe you could take a class.
CHRIS: Good idea.

Here, John got credit for a great idea that wasn't his at all, it was Chris'. This technique can be especially effective with Extroverts who tend to appreciate talking ideas through and sometimes just need a sounding board.

Acknowledge Agreement

There's one more part to showing empathy. Often, listeners don't acknowledge it when they agree with things others say. Agreeing with someone is a positive, and sometimes momentous, occasion. (In some negotiations, it's more momentous than others!) Make the most of this golden opportunity for camaraderie by letting them know you feel their statement is a gem.

You Can Never Agree Too Much

A question that usually comes up in seminars is how often should I express agreement? First, no one, not even our biggest fan, is going to agree with us always. We can tell the difference between sincerity and flattery. The answer is that you should outwardly show agreement by a nod, a smile, a spoken affirmation, anything—as much as you want to—as long as it's sincere.

Psychologists call this positive reinforcement. In fact, an entire field of psychology called behaviorism is built around the notion that animals, including humans, seek positive reinforcement. We seek it from our friends, our families, our spouses, our bosses, and the people we're negotiating with.

Positive Reinforcement Comes in Many Shapes and Sizes

There are many ways to show positive reinforcement. Injecting, "good idea," or "I've never thought if it that way," or "good point," or giving someone a standing ovation are all signs that say your ideas are good and your presence is valued. The key ingredient is that the praise must be genuine.

If you're the kind of person who will stand on a table and shout, "You are a genius," go for it. If you're the type that will stop someone in the hall after the meeting and quietly tell them, "That was a very constructive suggestion you made," that's just as good. No matter what your style, your sincerity will come through loud and clear, and your intention will be appreciated.

Positive reinforcement works. Negative reinforcement also affects the recipients, but usually works against those that employ it. Instead of making people feel treasured and wanted, negative reinforcement makes them feel unwanted and demoralized.

Take "Yes, But" Out of Your Vocabulary

"Yes, but" is, arguably, the single greatest negotiation wet blanket there is.[4] It causes negotiators to feel that they are not being listened to, or that their values are stupid or inferior.

This is such a waste, because often the intent of "yes, but" was never to belittle others. But that's the outcome, and here's how it happens:

> **CARL:** I think going to the movies would be fun.
> **GINNY:** Yes, but bowling would be better.

What Ginny meant	What Carl heard
Movies are a good idea. Right now bowling is better for me. I've been sitting all day and could use some exercise.	You think going to the movies is a stupid idea. You don't care about what I like, just your own ideas.

> **PETE:** If we are going to make our sales projections, we'll need to increase our marketing budget.
> **KIM:** Yes, but we need to purchase new computer equipment.

What Kim meant	What Pete heard
Marketing is important. So are capital equipment purchases.	You don't care if we make our sales projections. You just want to buy computers.

As you can see, "yes, but" leads to unnecessary misunderstandings. Another negotiation tactic that causes much frustration is the "Yes, But Game." After every suggestion there is a rapid fire "yes, but." Soon both players get frustrated dealing with each other and give up. Fortunately, "yes, but" is easy to cure. It only involves changing one word, and improves negotiations greatly.

Use "Yes, And" Instead of "Yes, But"

Negotiators who find themselves using "yes, but" can easily change their pattern. Wherever "yes, but" would go, substitute "Yes, and." Adding a supportive statement after the "yes" will further strengthen the message, "I'm listening to you and I appreciate what you are saying."[5] Here's how it works:

> **CARL:** I think going to the movies would be a good idea.
> **GINNY:** Yes, that's a good idea because there are lots of good movies out, *and* I want to go bowling so I can get some exercise.

<u>WHAT CARL HEARD:</u> My idea is appreciated by Ginny, and she has another idea worth considering.

> **PETE:** If we are going to make our sales projections, we'll need to increase our marketing budget.
> **KIM:** Increasing the marketing budget is a significant aspect of making our sales projections, *and* we have been delaying buying much needed computer equipment for a long time.

<u>WHAT PETE HEARD:</u> Kim thinks that increasing the marketing effort needs to happen because making the sales projections is essential. She also has concerns about delaying long-overdue computer purchases.

Appreciation Fosters a Cooperative Spirit

As you can see, what senders hear when "yes, but" is used is disdain, and they feel resentment. That feeling of resentment hampers negotiations because instead of focusing on issues, the parties focus on how much they annoy each other.

When senders hear "yes, and" they feel listened to, which leads to a willingness to discuss the issues. Also, since they are being listened to, their minds are open to hearing the other party. That feeling of cooperation will foster a collaborative spirit in negotiations. In the examples above, the parties still have to choose movies, bowling, advertising, or a computer. Since they are talking to each other they can develop solutions. (This will be covered in chapter 5, making proposals and handling objections.)

There is another word good negotiators avoid when they speak to others. That word is "you."

Good Negotiators Avoid Saying "You"

As mentioned before, the goal of a negotiation is concentrating effort on the problem, not the negotiators. Throwing "you" into a conversation puts the focal point of the negotiation on the personalities of the negotiators, instead of on the problem itself.

The destructive force of "you" cannot be overemphasized. For example, "I can't believe you think that," or "you really don't know what you're talking about," or "you need to check your facts."

These personal attacks generally lead to bitterness or a return personal attack. After a few volleys, the negotiation can break down to nothing but a shouting session, with very little focus on the problem.

Sometimes it's not easy to tell when the negotiators aren't crazy about each other. Diplomats have their special euphemisms for hostile negotiations. This way, the two parties can call each other names and still give the appearance of civility. When the spokesperson reports on how the negotiations are going says:

> "The two parties met and had a frank and open discussion covering a wide range of topics. The groundwork was laid for more substantive talks."

The translation is:

> "The two parties yelled at each other a lot. Instead of talking about the issues, they insulted each other. With any luck, they'll get something accomplished tomorrow."

The moral of the story is that saying nice words isn't enough. You have to mean them, too.

Instead of "You," Use Impersonal Terms

Good negotiators know it's counterproductive to rile the other party. Lobbing potshots may bring a small, immediate victory, but it stalls the negotiation, causing long-term losses. Don't say "you," be impersonal.

Instead of	Say
Are you going to sign the agreement?	When is the agreement going to be signed?
Do you understand this yet?	Is the material clear?
Are you thick? *or* Are you stupid?	What has not been clearly explained?

The questions on the left focus on the person. The receiver can counterattack, melt, leave, or parry the attack. When people are asked something as charged as, "Are you thick?" they always respond, although the response may be simply getting angry or walking away.

The questions on the right focus instead on the problem. The receiver will not feel personally threatened so will react in a non-threatening way. When receivers hear, "What has not been clearly explained?" they won't feel under attack and will continue to work to resolve a conflict.

Another characteristic of the statements on the right is that they are sincere questions, another major negotiation ingredient. That will be looked at in detail in chapter 3.

Conclusion

At the start of the negotiation process, both parties have concerns, and both want solutions. Although they may have differing concerns, they're trying to come to an agreeable solution. Solutions that work are the ones in which both parties win.

Communication is the start of the negotiation process and will be the medium by which ideas are exchanged. Introverts and Extroverts communicate in different ways. They are:

The Introvert/Extrovert Preference

Introvert doesn't mean "shy" and Extrovert doesn't mean "bold." Roughly speaking, Introverts think to themselves, and Extroverts think aloud. Here's a breakdown.

Introvert	Extrovert
Wants time for reflection.	Wants to talk about solutions.
Finds meetings draining.	Finds being alone draining.
Thinks before speaking.	Thinks while speaking.

When you're negotiating, make sure communication is proceeding smoothly. Avoid "yes, but" and use "yes, and" instead.

NOTES

1. Isabel Briggs Myers and Mary H. McCaulley, *Manual: A Guide to the Development and Use of the Myers-Briggs Type Indicator* (Palo Alto, Calif.: Consulting Psychologists Press, 1985), 244.
2. Myers and McCaulley, *Manual: A Guide to MBTI*, 244–246.
3. David Keirsey and Marilyn Bates, *Please Understand Me: Character and Temperament Types* (Del Mar, Calif.: Prometheus Nemesis Books: 1978), 14.
4. Susan M. Heitler, *From Conflict to Resolution: Strategies for Diagnosis and Treatment of Distressed Individuals, Couples and Families.* (New York: Norton, 1990), 305–306.
5. Heitler, *From Conflict to Resolution*, 111.

Chapter 4
PERSONALITY NEGOTIATING
IS THE TRANSLATOR

Communicating is the first piece in the negotiation puzzle. If one person speaks French and another Italian, knowing about the Introvert/Extrovert preference discussed in the last chapter becomes nothing more than an academic exercise.

Non-communication happens when people speak the same language, too. Just ask any teenager and/or parent of one if you have doubts.

One reason communication breaks down in negotiations is that negotiators often see the same data, idea, object, or circumstance very differently. Seeing the same thing differently isn't inherently bad. The advantage of a diversity of ideas is that the amalgamation of thought, like a hybrid crop, often yields a better, stronger final product. Often, participants leave the negotiation with a different but positive perception of the needs of the other side.

The potential downside of an assortment of opinions is seen when negotiators leave the negotiation and proceed to bang their heads against the wall. They feel that they aren't being understood and don't have a clue what the other side is trying to say.

Have you ever noticed that some meetings are boring, while others are more interesting? The meetings that keep our attention are the ones that key in on our personality type, while the dull ones are those that don't.

Interestingly, we tend to present data the way we would want data presented to us. This strategy only works with those who think as we do. Since you negotiate with a variety of people with a variety of personality types (sometimes seated at the very same negotiating table) you'll need to adapt your style accordingly.

Obviously, you want to make the most of any negotiation. The key is knowing the type of information you and others prefer and why. This is covered for you in the second Personality Negotiating preference. It examines how people view evidence and ideas presented during the negotiation. It is this Sensing/Intuitive preference that we are looking at next.

The Sensing/Intuitive Index

The next critical area of Personality Negotiating is the Sensing/Intuitive index. This is useful when you make a presentation, or give supporting evidence. Sensates and Intuitives differ greatly in the way they look at things, and how they want proof shown to them.

To illustrate the significant difference between Sensates and Intuitives, put an apple on the table and ask someone to "list all the words that describe your concept of an apple."

Sensates use their five senses to describe the apple. They tell you how it looks, feels, tastes, the sound it makes when you bite into it, etc.

Intuitives use their imagination and tell you what associations they link with the apple. They'll say computers (Apple computers), Hallowe'en, New York, William Tell, Adam and Eve, grandmother's house, etc., but may never mention that the apple is red. Although they know it's red, they won't list it because it's not important to them.

The Sensates describe the apple on the table, while the Intuitives describe apples in general. Here's a breakdown of what each type looks for.

Sensing	Intuitive
Wants the facts.	Wants the concept.
Needs the practicality.	Likes innovations.
Needs the details.	Doesn't want details.

Details and facts are very important to Sensates. According to Robert Benfari, Ph.D., of Harvard University's School of Public Health, "If you give a Sensate a balance sheet, he'll add it up. If you give that same balance sheet to an Intuitive, he'll make a business plan."

The most striking aspect of the Sensing/Intuitive preference when Personality Negotiating is that Sensates need the details of a proposal before they can understand how the solution benefits them. They'll think that solutions without factual data to back them up or details that prove a point are meaningless. Sensates prefer written reports rich in facts that they can analyze.

Intuitives Are Different

Intuitives, on the other hand, need to have the big picture first—details up front will be trivial to them. Intuitives will think that presentations are tedious and boring if there are too many facts and details. That's why Intuitives prefer charts and graphs with the big picture in mind.

Of course, Introverted Sensates and Intuitives like having reports they can read alone, while Extroverted Sensates and Intuitives prefer to talk abut the written material.

Which type are you? If you're interested, answer the following questions:

DIRECTIONS: Read each of these eleven items and circle answer A or B, depending on which response fits you best. There are no right, wrong, or better answers. You'll find information on calculating your preference at the end of the test.

1. **You are most convinced by:**
   A) a presentation with a strong overview.
   B) a presentation with a lot of facts.
2. **When learning a new concept, a lot of details first:**
   A) are overwhelming.
   B) are essential to understanding.
3. **When describing something, you usually:**
   A) describe it literally.
   B) describe it conceptually.
4. **If someone gave you a proposal on inexpensive paper, you would:**
   A) probably not notice it or be bothered by it.
   B) view that negatively.
5. **You tend to:**
   A) notice little things.
   B) not notice little things.
6. **You like buying things that are:**
   A) the latest and greatest.
   B) tried and true.
7. **You find untried, new ideas:**
   A) sometimes interesting, but often unworkable.
   B) interesting and useful.
8. **When you make a decision, you most want to know:**
   A) how it benefits you immediately.
   B) how it fits into future plans.
9. **You are swayed more by how:**
   A) concepts relate to facts.
   B) facts relate to concepts.
10. **When faced with a new problem with no predetermined rules and regulations, you would:**
    A) work within the rules established for other company programs, using accepted company procedures.

B) think of as many solutions to the problem as possible, despite the established rules.
11. **You prefer to think of yourself as a:**
    A) pragmatist.
    B) dreamer.

SCORING:
Add the **A** answers for questions
3, 5, 7, 8, 10, 11
Add the **B** answers for questions
1, 2, 4, 6, 9

Put the Total here:_____ **S/N**

If the Total is 6 or more, you're most likely **Sensing.** Otherwise, you're most likely an **Intuitive.**

Occupations Common to Sensates and Intuitives

Here's a list of occupations that have a predominance of Sensates and Intuitives.[1] Again, every profession has a mix of personality types. (All accountants aren't Sensates, all actors aren't Intuitive.)

Sensates Predominantly	Intuitives Predominantly
banker	journalist
manager	manager
accountant	marketing
insurance executive	lawyer
office manager	cleric
teacher (high school)	professor (college)
engineer	social worker
executive	psychologist
military personnel	actor

Manager shows up twice because that is a position held by a high predominance of both Sensing and Intuitive types.

When you negotiate, make sure you know what type others are so you can adjust your presentation to them. Sensates and Intuitives expect a far different type of presentation, so find out which they want as soon as you can.

Preparing for the Negotiation

Now that you understand the type of evidence and supporting data to use during a negotiation, here are specific steps to insure the negotiation meeting flows smoothly.

Before we go on, a brief word on the setting where the negotiations will take place. Sometimes it is a conference room, but it can also be a brief conversation in the halls, at the copy machine, at lunch, or in someone's office. Many of the techniques that are useful in meeting-type negotiations are transferable to more informal types.

A good way to find out about the Sensing/Intuitive preferences of the people you're negotiating with is to have a meeting before the formal negotiations begin. This prevents surprises that can sometimes creep up during the meeting.

Step 1: Have a Pre-Meeting Meeting

A pre-meeting meeting is the perfect forum for informal give and take. The way it works is that you call strategic people you'll be meeting with and talk over your and their concerns. In the following example, Mike wants to run a computer program on the company's mainframe that will print out 20,000 labels for marketing mailings each month. He has sent his proposal to Ed Junction, the Management Information Systems director. Here, Mike calls Ed before the meeting to discuss the proposal:

> **MIKE:** I wanted to call you to see what you think of our proposal before the departmental meeting.
>
> **ED:** Thanks for calling. I have a few concerns about the amount of time your program is going to take on our computer.
>
> **MIKE:** What's your concern?
>
> **ED:** Our end-of-month transaction processing takes twenty-four hours and uses both of our laser printers. I don't think the computer can take any more processing during that time.
>
> **MIKE:** Our label program doesn't need to run at the end of the month. What if we ran it on the fifteenth instead?
>
> **ED:** That would be okay. Why don't you present that time line during the meeting and I'll give the idea my support.

Since the pre-meeting conversation is low-stress, you're free to make proposals that might otherwise be difficult to make in a meeting. This is especially true if you are dealing with Sensing types since Sensing types find it difficult to discuss possibilities without much supporting proof to analyze them. However, providing the details before the formal meeting will give the Sensing types plenty of time to look at anything you think is critical for them to be familiar with.

When you negotiate with Introverts, make sure to send them materials a week before the meeting if possible so that they can review them before your arrival. If they're Extroverts, call them and tell them what you're planning to present so that you can get verbal feedback. If you're unsure if they are Introverts or Extroverts, then say, "I have a few ideas I'd like you to review before the meeting. Would you like to discuss them or should I send them to you?"

The Introverts will want to review the ideas privately, while the Extroverts will want to discuss the ideas with you.

Other Benefits of Pre-Meeting Conversations

Pre-meeting conversations have other benefits, too. You've started a personal relationship that is low-stress because you didn't actually ask them to make a commitment. If the upcoming meeting is a group negotiation, then you can count on at least one person who will support you during the meeting. At least one person will champion, or support, your ideas. During the meeting your champion will handle the objections of other group members much more vociferously than you can, and will act as your agent. Why? Because of your pre-sales conversation, your champion has taken partial ownership of your ideas. He'll advocate your ideas for you because it's not just your solution now, it's coming from both of you.

At the Meeting—Be Prepared

Before the meeting starts, make sure that you have your presentation materials, that your audio-visual equipment is working, that the audio-visuals themselves can be seen easily from every seat, and, most importantly, that you know what you want to accomplish during the meeting.

Step 2: Begin the Meeting

If you are running the meeting, make sure that everyone is introduced. Then get a consensus from the group about what should be accomplished.

Step 3: Establish and Review Goals

At the beginning of the meeting review your and others' goals and expectations. You might say,

> "First, I'd like to review the action items we had from the last meeting. Next, I'd like to review the sales figures from last quarter. Finally, we'll review the forecast for the fourth quarter and decide on an advertising budget. Would anyone like to add something?"

Write suggestions down—if possible on a white board or a flip chart. This clearly shows that you are listening and intend to deal with any concerns voiced.

Someone might say:

> "If we are going to increase the advertising, we'll need to beef up the sales support staff to handle the increased call load."
> "Good point. I'll add it to the agenda."

An Intuitive audience wants detailed answers after the overview:

> "I'll cover that after the proposal. Is that okay?"

Sensing audiences want questions taken immediately:

> "That's a good question. I'll go over that now."

What Are the Goals of a Negotiation Meeting?

Negotiations have many different goals. Every meeting won't have all the objectives listed below, but each will have one or several of them:

- Introduce one another
- Gather information
- Answer objections
- Present information
- Demonstrate a solution
- Prove a point
- Reach an agreement
- Handle a crisis
- Explain a position
- Hear complaints
- Complain
- Tell clients what you're doing for them

- Meet key members of the company
- Show the people you represent that you are working toward a solution

Step 4: Find Out If Group Wants a Sensing or Intuitive Presentation

No matter what the goals of the meeting are, Sensing meetings start with details and Intuitive meetings start with overviews. If there's a consensus on first giving details or overviews, proceed. If not, give some details during an overview. Direct the details to the Sensing members and the overviews to Intuitive members.

> "Most would like the details first. Okay. The plan as I see it is to increase our direct mailing by 30 percent. This should bring in about an extra 3,000 leads. This is based on a historically proven 2 percent response rate with the lists we use. [This is for the Sensates.] Here is a chart showing expected revenue increases due to the larger mailing. [This is for the Intuitives.]"

Sensates get the details and practicality that they need, and the Intuitives get the quick overview they need. Switching between Sensing and Intuitive presentation styles for mixed groups insures that everyone understands and appreciates your presentations.

Step 5: Make the Presentation

Sometimes, during the negotiation, you're going to have to present your concerns or ideas to a group instead of one person. Sometimes you can avoid a large presentation and stick to one-to-one meetings, but that's not always feasible or a good use of your or their time.

Most of us don't like speaking in front of a group. In fact, *The Book of Lists* puts public speaking as Americans' greatest fear. This is ahead of snakes, heights, and dying. Here are some tips to make your presentation effective, whether you like making presentations or not:

1. **The best performances happen during nervousness.** More world records are broken in the Olympics than at any other time. This is because athletes perform best when their adrenaline is flowing. Speakers are the same way—their best performances come when they're in the heat of the spotlight.
2. **You're not the entertainment.** You are presenting to provide insights to people who need to hear them. Many presentations in a negotiation aren't in the engaging category, anyway. Being yourself is all that anyone can ask. If you find joking during a presentation natural, that's fine—as long as the situation warrants it.

Professional comedians say the toughest part of their act is the first joke because, if the first joke bombs, they have a hard time winning over the audience. Starting off with a joke is like betting on a long shot that pays even money. The risk of losing the audience is great, and the payoff is low.

3. **Don't apologize.** People expect to like a presentation before they hear it. Often, one has to work very hard to prove them wrong. The exception is when speakers apologize for how bad their presentation will be before they start. Audiences tend to believe and down-rate a speaker who says, "I'm not very good at speaking, and you're probably going to be bored." However, if that speaker had simply started the presentation, the audience would have thought he or she did just fine.

4. **Know your subject area well.** You don't have to be an expert, but you do need to have a working knowledge of your area. Too, you've got to establish credibility immediately. Using your knowledge and experience, as quickly as you can you must convince your audience that you know what you're talking about. The group will listen to you if they think they can benefit from what you say.

   If speakers can't answer basic questions (different from knowing everything), Sensing members of the audience will assume they are unqualified. Intuitive audiences will come to the same conclusion, only more slowly.

   If you don't know an answer, don't make one up. Sensates, especially, will express their confusion when details or facts don't add up. (Don't think they are being belligerent, they are probably genuinely confused.) If your educated guesses aren't working, you'll quickly find yourself tap dancing.

   Ask if an audience member knows the answer—often one will. If the answer isn't immediately available, no one's going to think less of you if you have to check your facts before you give a response.

5. **Maintain eye contact with the audience.** This will enhance your credibility (a common perception is, if you don't look them in the eye, you're not trustworthy) and keep the audience's attention on you. Avoid scanning the audience, or looking over their heads.

   The above is true of American audiences. Foreign audiences are different. Japanese negotiators will view it a sign of disrespect if you look them in the eye. Middle Eastern negotiators will want to be a few inches from your face. A good rule of thumb, if you're involved in international or intercultural negotiations, is to check out such behavioral customs before you start.

6. **Don't ramble.** Once you've made a statement, don't keep repeating it. This is different from reviewing main points.
7. **Don't fidget.** Many speakers swear that they don't tap pens or shift from foot to foot while speaking—until they see themselves doing so on videotape. These idiosyncrasies are distracting to the audience.
8. **Review main points.** Tell the audience the main areas you want to cover and, as each topic has been presented, remind them of the main points and any conclusions that may have been reached.
9. **Make sure your audio-visuals are right.**

Step 6: Explain That You Want Everyone to Win

As was mentioned last chapter, you want to stress that the ultimate outcome of the meeting is to have everyone come out a winner.

Step 7: Ask Sincere Questions

A sincere question is one that you don't know the answer to, but need to get a person's response to to understand the person you're negotiating with, or their position. A rule in negotiations is that sincere questions are always appropriate. A corollary to that principle is that sincere questions will have sincere responses.

> "You said you're unhappy with your job. Could you tell me why? I want to know so we can work out a plan to make you happier."

Insincere questions, on the other hand, are questions you know the answer to, or use to verbally manipulate, attack, or belittle the person you're negotiating with. Lawyers learn in law school never to ask a question they don't know the answer to. They also learn that making adversaries appear stupid and themselves appear smart wins points with clients.

> "You say you're unhappy in your job . . . could you define happiness in this context? . . . What you're saying is that we are not entertaining enough for you . . . perhaps we could have a clown perform a private show for you several times a day, would that make your job more entertaining?"

Negotiators aren't lawyers. Unless the goal is negotiating someone into prison, stick to sincere questions.

Forms of Insincerity

There are as many forms of insincerity as there are insincere people. Insincere people don't do very well in negotiations because they tend to be concerned with one-upsmanship and not with working on collaborative solutions. Instead of the Win–Win deal, they are looking for what educator Ellen Saisi calls the "I-Win deal." Chapter 11, Negotiating with Difficult People, will cover, in detail, how to deal with those who attempt to win at your expense.

How is insincerity conveyed? Some unintentional ways are listed above. Here are some overt ways:

> **What they say:** This is far too complex for you. It's technical.
>
> **What they mean:** You are far too stupid to grasp something that only someone with my intelligence and technical capabilities could understand. Even trying to explain it to you would be a waste of time.

> **What they say:** I don't have time to listen to you. (When they do have time.)
>
> **What they mean:** Anything you have to say will be of no use to me.

> **What they say:** Do you expect me to believe that?
> **What they mean:** You are lying to make a point.

As you know, when people insult our competence or character, negotiation grinds to a screeching halt. We all, at times, have thought about saying something mean to those who are annoying. It's human nature to want to occasionally put people in their place.

In these instances, getting teeth marks on our tongue from biting back the remark is the wise alternative. Jabbing with a cutting remark will win a temporary victory in the superiority game, but impedes the progress of the negotiation. Discretion, they say, is the better part of valor. It also keeps negotiations moving in the right direction, focusing on the issues, instead of tending to wounds caused by insults and insincerity.

Sincere questions glean the merit and concerns of the people you negotiate with. It's crucial that others understand you, too. That's covered next.

Step 8: Educate Others on Your Concern's Merit

If you're negotiating with a skilled questioner, your job is much easier. They'll probe for your concerns and find out what's important to you. When others don't know which of your concerns are high priorities, it's up to you to educate them.

A negotiation without the other side's having a complete grasp of your concerns is like a balance that is weighted unequally—one side is going to tip. The first thing you need to do is to impress on them that the success of the negotiation hinges on understanding:

PHIL: I understand your concerns now. Knowing your concerns is very useful to me because without a clear picture of what you want, I can't develop a mutually beneficial solution. Now I'll explain my concerns so that we'll have all the information we need to negotiate.

Notice how Phil mentioned that understanding concerns was key to a mutually beneficial agreement? He is setting the stage for cooperation. When one-sided proposals come to the table, Phil can say, "I can't accept that because it isn't mutually beneficial." If it's a good deal, he can say, "We should take this deal because it benefits both of us." Using a win–win strategy to counter an offer will be covered in detail in chapter 5.

After others recognize that understanding your concerns is vital to the success of the negotiation, you can begin presenting them. Try to think of as many issues as possible that they must know for you to come out a winner.

Sometimes people feel comfortable hearing others' concerns, but self-conscious expressing their own. If this is the case: 1) remember that this is a crucial piece of the negotiation; 2) the agreement will be stronger for both of you because of it; and 3) express issues in impersonal rather than personal terms.

IMPERSONAL: Having more office staff available on Fridays is necessary to handle the additional work due to the end-of-week reports that need to get done.
PERSONAL TERMS: We really need help on Fridays because we are so busy, and everyone gets frazzled because of the deadlines.

Sometimes the educational process is rocky. This is true especially when you're dealing with extreme versions of personality types. Here, proceed with caution.

Intuitives and Sensates Taken to the Extreme

The strength in the Intuitives preference is that they see possibilities and are adept at developing plans. Sensates complement Intuitives by determining which of many possible ideas are practical. Sensates save

Intuitives' time by helping them avoid inevitable dead ends. Intuitives help Sensates by exploring the roads less travelled and discovering gems along the way.

When these positive qualities are in the extreme, however, negotiations can be grueling. Extreme Sensates refuse to consider any new idea, conduct meetings that laboriously trudge through details of only peripheral, if any, significance, demand that documents contain every detail on a problem, when only a summary would suffice.

Extreme Intuitives want to focus on future problems instead of current ones, will pursue unworkable ideas, will shun practicality in times of austerity, and will refuse to absorb essential details that are critical to a decision. Negotiations with extremes are difficult, but not impossible.

When Dealing with an Extreme

When dealing with an extreme personality type, remember that, in general, extreme types are trying to be helpful, not difficult. This is sometimes a hard view to maintain while you're pulling your hair out. When dealing with supreme Sensates, tell them that you appreciate their attention to detail, but that level of preciseness is not necessary at this time.

> "I appreciate your wanting to fill us in on the minutes of the last meeting. Since we were all there, and we have only one hour, I think time would best be spent moving forward with the current issues. Why don't you type up your notes and distribute them after the meeting?"

If you're dealing with intense Intuitives, tell them that you appreciate their creativity and their concern with future problems, but that the focus of the negotiation needs to be the problems at hand.

> "Your solutions are dynamic and exciting, and I think that efforts here would be best spent on solutions that will fit into our current year's budget. I'll set up a meeting for you with the head of R&D next week."

Of course, Sensates and Intuitives always see just about anything differently. It's not surprising they learn in various ways, too.

There Will Always Be Diversity

The fact that negotiators learn differently isn't surprising, because anything from algebra to the zone defense is grasped at different rates, and in different ways, too. While diversity of ideas can bring strength, it often brings contempt and hampers understanding and agreement.

The Sensing/Intuitive preference explains one reason why people have difficulty understanding each other—we absorb knowledge in very specific ways. The next chapter explains how concerns are generated from ideas or situations and how to address them.

Conclusion

Formal negotiating meetings are useful, but much negotiation goes on behind the scenes when ideas can be bandied about more freely. In formal negotiations, whether you're talking to one person or a group, structure your negotiation to the audience's personality and address concerns according to their personality types. Doing this makes handling concerns and wrapping up the negotiation, which will be covered in the next chapters, easier.

For successful negotiation interactions, follow the following steps:

STEP 1: Do pre-negotiation test marketing of your ideas.

STEP 2: Establish the goals of the meeting.

STEP 3: Find out if the group at the bargaining table wants a Sensing or Intuitive presentation.

STEP 4: Make the presentation.

Negotiating with Sensates

<u>BEHAVIOR</u>: Sensates trust detailed evidence they have collected or analyzed themselves. They tend to be conservative and rely on facts. They prefer written proposals to verbal ones.

<u>WHAT TO WATCH OUT FOR</u>: Sensates lose confidence in the entire proposal if they find typos or inaccurate data. If the presentation has a messy appearance, Sensates will be distracted by what you say. Many Sensates will assume that carelessness was the reason for any inaccuracies and reason that, if you were careless with the presentation, you don't care about their concerns. If doing a highly detailed, pristine-looking proposal is difficult for you, you're probably an Intuitive. Have a Sensate, who finds detailed proposals natural and easy to do, help you.

New ideas need to be approached with caution since Sensates are more comfortable with established, tried, and proven ideas. Sensates want practical, realistic products that are in their budget. They like structure and procedures, and will make responsible buying decisions.

Negotiating with Intuitives

BEHAVIOR: Intuitives can become overwhelmed with details and prefer overviews. When faced with a decision, Intuitives will want to analyze as many solutions as possible.

WHAT TO WATCH OUT FOR: Intuitives will consider solutions that don't appear practical. Intuitives may explore unworkable possibilities. If their exploration is an obstacle, help them get back on track.

Intuitives love discussing innovative ideas and creative possibilities. Don't be afraid that a solution is "way out." Intuitives like charts and graphs that show the big picture. If you feel your proposals have too many details for your customer, you're probably a Sensate. Show your proposal to an Intuitive first and have him or her help you.

Presenting to Various Types

INTROVERTS want materials they can read by themselves. They prefer one-to-one meetings and they consider phone calls and unscheduled visits to be interruptions.

EXTROVERTS like to talk about solutions and like discussing ideas in groups or committees. They consider unscheduled visits and phone calls welcome diversions.

SENSING types want to know details and facts. They'll want to go over each line in your proposal. Extroverted Sensing types will want to talk about every detail of the proposal.

Introverted Sensing types will want to analyze the proposal privately. They prefer written presentations rich in documented data from reliable sources. The proposal should be neatly organized and free of spelling and calculation errors.

INTUITIVES will want to know how ideas and proposals will affect the entire company and the future ramifications of the decision they'll be making. Details will be unimportant until the final stages of a decision. Charts and graphs looked at macroscopically will be appreciated.

NOTE

1. Myers and McCaulley, *Manual: A Guide to MBTI*, 246–248.

Chapter 5
PERSONALITY NEGOTIATING ADDRESSES CONCERNS

People negotiate for different reasons, and in accordance with different personal values. Ultimately, the decisions reached during any negotiation reflect the personalities of the participants. If the outcome doesn't meld with long-term goals, then the accords reached are doomed to a short life or failure.

So far, the book has covered how communication and understanding improve negotiation. This chapter covers that part of a negotiation when the sides make proposals and counter-proposals. With proposals come responses, and those responses can be positive, negative, or neutral. No matter what type of negotiation you're conducting, you can turn the lukewarm to cold reactions into collaborative agreements.

You, of course, are familiar with the types of negotiation that take place when you buy something, like a car. Salespeople make proposals to you that, as the customer, are yours to accept or reject. Though communication between you and the salesperson is two-way, the direction of cash flows only one way: you fork over the cash, and salespeople the goods.

Non-sales negotiations happen in a far different atmosphere. Each negotiator constantly vacillates between the role of deal-seller and deal-accepter. As the deal-seller, you want your contributions to be taken. As the deal-accepter, you strive to arrive at fair solutions. Fair agreements are the ones with staying power because those are the ones people put their efforts into carrying out, rather than spending time searching for loopholes.

"No, Thanks"

Negotiators refuse offers when they have unaddressed concerns, or for some other reason are not ready to make a commitment. This chapter is going to outline the types of concerns people have, and how to constructively settle concerns you and others may have.

To explain why people are reluctant to make commitments during negotiations, let's look at the third area of Personality Negotiating, the Thinking/Feeling index. This preference measures what people value in making decisions.

The Thinking/Feeling Index

The third area of Personality Negotiating is the Thinking/Feeling index. This index concerns what motivates people to decide and how these individuals relate to others.

Thinking types view people and things analytically and objectively. Feeling types view people and things personally and emotionally, while Thinking types tend to find it easy to think of groups impersonally. Feeling types view groups as a collection of individuals. They want to improve people's lives. Thinking types, on the other hand, are motivated by logic.

If you're interested in what type you are, answer the following questions:

DIRECTIONS: Read each of the eleven items and circle answer A or B, depending on which response fits you best. There are no right, wrong, or better answers. You'll find information on scoring the test at the end of the test.

1. **If you make a decision, you are usually swayed by:**
   A) how you're sure it will turn out.
   B) how you hope it will turn out.
2. **If you are buying something for someone else, you are concerned:**
   A) that you are buying the right thing.
   B) that they will like it.
3. **You like dealing with people who are:**
   A) nice.
   B) predictable.
4. **When you buy something, you are more concerned with:**
   A) its cost.
   B) how much people will like it.
5. **When you think about several people with much in common you tend to think of them:**
   A) as individuals.
   B) as a group.
6. **If you're in a negotiation and two people are arguing, you:**
   A) feel uncomfortable that there is disharmony.
   B) assume that interpersonal conflict is unavoidable.

7. **If your company has a layoff that you know will be financially difficult for some employees, you would:**
   A) feel bad for those being laid off.
   B) assume that layoffs are unfortunate, but inevitable.
8. **If someone complains about your boss, you would:**
   A) not take it personally.
   B) take it personally.
9. **After trying with no luck to make a disgruntled person happy, you would:**
   A) keep trying until you are successful.
   B) give up.
10. **Your best buying decisions were made:**
    A) rationally and precisely.
    B) emotionally.
11. **You tend to be a person who makes decisions that are:**
    A) consistent.
    B) based on extenuating circumstances.

SCORING:
Add the **A** answers for questions
1, 2, 4, 8, 10, 11
Add the **B** answers for questions
3, 5, 6, 7, 9

Put the Total here:_____ **T/F**

If the Total is 6 or more you're most likely a **Thinking** type, otherwise you're most likely a **Feeling** type.

Occupations Common to Thinking and Feeling Types

Here's a list of occupations commonly chosen by Thinking and Feeling types.[1]

Thinking Types Predominate	Feeling Types Predominate
manager	cleric
researcher	preschool teacher
programmer	receptionist
auditor	nurse
banker	office manager
credit investigator	librarian

steel worker	waiter/waitress
scientist	counselor
engineer	physician
detective	musician

Thinking types' concerns usually focus on an option not making sense or the internal cost/benefit analysis not measuring up. You address Thinking types' concerns by giving them analytical proof that your idea is the best and logical choice.

Feeling types' concerns will be put in terms of a proposal not enhancing someone's life, or an expected emotionally difficult transition period. You manage their concerns by showing them that your solution makes life easier or better. You do this by either having the Feeling types talk to references or by doing a trial. The references will tell the Feeling types that others are happy with your ideas, that they have been successful elsewhere. A trial is a pressure-free method that allows the Feeling type to see first-hand how your proposal will benefit people important to them.

Typing the Thinking or Feeling Negotiator

By listening and observing you can find out if the people you are negotiating with are Thinking or Feeling types. Ask them, "What are your decision-making criteria?"

If they say things like, "I want it to be efficient," or "If they don't like it, screw 'em," they're Thinking types. Unless you can show that bliss directly affects the end result, don't push it.

If they say, "I won't decide until I'm convinced that my staff will be happy," they're Feeling types. Pushing cost-savings or efficiency will have limited impact because Feeling types view these types of advantages as much lower priorities than human benefit.

Negotiating with Thinking Types

Here's how to handle the concerns of Thinking types:

THINKING TYPE: Paying middle managers $50,000 a year is ridiculous. When I was at their level, I was making half that and I didn't complain.

Focus your reply on the logical elements answering this concern.

RESPONSE: When you were a middle manager twenty years ago, cars were selling for $3,000, and houses cost a third of what they do today. The middle managers of today at $50,000 are, relatively speaking, making as much or less than you did twenty years ago.

Handling Concerns of Feeling Types

When Feeling types have concerns, focus on the benefits people will derive from the negotiation.

FEELING TYPE: The middle managers are always asking for more money. Can't they just get satisfaction from a job well done?

RESPONSE: Our managers do care abut their jobs, but people work for financial reasons as well as emotional ones. If we didn't pay people, no one would be here.

———————————

Three of the four areas of Personality Negotiating have been covered so far: Introvert/Extrovert, Sensing/Intuitive, and Thinking/Feeling. The Thinking/Feeling preference determines how we generate concerns internally.

Resolving Concerns by Type

Preferences work in combination. The way an Introverted Intuitive Feeling type expresses or resolves concerns will be very different from the way an Extroverted Sensing Feeling type reconciles concerns. Let's look at how to address concerns of personality combinations we've looked at so far.

Introvert/Extrovert

Extroverts tell you their concerns without prompting, while Introverts wait for you to ask what their concerns are. So often, Introverts silently stew about a situation, letting it fester until someone asks them if anything's bothering them. Don't assume that silence equals happiness because it often doesn't. In negotiations, silence is not golden—especially with Introverts. When unhappy Introverts are asked if they have concerns, they are likely to share quite a bit! To make sure there aren't any unspoken concerns, ask non-threatening questions designed to ferret out deeply held thoughts, such as:

"What are you thinking about? If we decided on these specs, would you be completely happy?"

Don't be surprised to hear:

"No. After reviewing the specs and data from previous meetings, I feel that the inexpensive materials we'd be recommending are substandard and would deteriorate in two years."

Sensing/Intuitive

Sensing types want practical and reliable outcomes supported with details and facts. Take an active role in providing that evidence. You could say:

"If you're worried about the turnaround time for the artwork in the ad, why don't we have someone with Graphics join us now?"

There are many ways to solve the problem of getting the Sensate relevant facts. Start the information gathering before he or she leaves. If reaching an agreement is important to you, do as much of the legwork as the negotiation dictates. This prevents procrastination, which often happens when people are left to tie up loose ends on their own. Getting hold of an expert who has the answer is often the quickest and easiest way to proceed. If an Introvert feels that there are many people to call to get answers, make the calls for him or her. If the negotiation is important, it will be worth your effort. If the expert can't meet with both of you, let the Sensate know how to contact the other party for verification.

"I spoke with Cherry Bamberg in our graphics department about turnaround time for the ad. She said she could start work on it this afternoon and have it ready tomorrow. If you have any questions, Cherry said feel free to call her at extension 417."

Though Introverted Sensing types prefer written information, it isn't always possible to get reliable data in that form. Think of as many ways as you can to get them needed answers that they will fully grasp and understand. If in doubt, ask them what they want.

Remember not to bluff the Sensate with details or facts that you aren't absolutely certain of. Their minds tend to work like huge computer databases, and they can retrieve large caches of knowledge very quickly.

People who try to make up facts as they go along will quickly find themselves treading water.

Intuitives, on the other hand, simply want to know how what you're proposing fits into their plans and they don't want lots of detailed analysis:

> "This chart shows how you'll save money over the next five years."

Thinking/Feeling

Thinking types like logical plans.

> "See how this works?" "How does this compare to other ideas you've considered?"

Feeling types want harmony when change is necessary.

> "Let's have your staff try out the computers to make sure they like the color monitors."

What If You Can't Answer All the Concerns?

Since you can't be all things to all people, there will be some concerns you can't answer. If this is the case—and all options have been looked at—honestly explain that you can't deliver exactly what they want.

> "I know that parking is tight, but we don't have the budget to build a garage."

When You Have Concerns

As mentioned in the previous chapter, in a negotiation there are two forces to reckon with, and you're one of them. Successful agreements not only have to be acceptable to the people you're dealing with, they have to be appropriate for you, too.

For Every Action, an Equal and Opposite Reaction

One of Isaac Newton's principles of motion is, "For every action, there is an equal and opposite reaction." That rings true for negotiation as well as for physics. Benevolent actions are met with benevolent responses, while destructive actions are met with equally destructive responses. (See chapter 9 for why this is so.)

If the people you're negotiating with take more than is fair, then you are getting less than is right for you. If you give away too much in a negotiation, then you're left with an unsatisfactory arrangement. Conversely, if you get more than your fair share, you'll likely end up with a bad deal, too. Fortunately, there is a way to come out ahead, and preserve relationships.

Using Win–Win to Address Concerns

When people are throwing out alternatives that are not favorable to you, but heavily weighted toward them, reject suggestions that don't adhere to a win–win philosophy.

If you've laid the groundwork for a win-win deal (covered in chapter 4), great. It's going to make your job much easier. Succinctly, this is what the other side will have heard:

> "I'm looking to reach an agreement in which we all win. If I get too much, and you lose, that's not good because you'll try to get out of the agreement. The same is true for me. If we come out with an agreement that isn't good for anyone, then we'll both lose. If I feel that I'm getting too much, I won't accept the agreement because I know that later you'll just keep to the letter of the contract, or try to get out of the agreement—anyhow a long-term relationship will be ended."

Now you're in the position to reject proposals based on unfairness. Here's how it works. Early on and throughout the negotiation, if there are suggestions made that benefit you, but not them, saying something to the effect of:

> "I can't accept that because I'd be winning and you'd be losing. Win–lose deals eventually disintegrate and are unacceptable to me."

That establishes your credibility and sincerity. If they present an option that's lose–win (you lose, they win) then you can adamantly reject their proposal for the same reasons:

> "Your suggestions would be a lose–win situation with my losing because I would have to increase my inventory with no guarantee of sales. Let's look at something else."

What you're doing is training people to be collaborative negotiators. The training works because you've done the groundwork, stressing the value of win–win up front.

They Agreed to a Win–Win Deal

Early in the negotiation, there was consensus that the goal of the negotiation was to have everyone come out a winner. Only the most difficult people (covered in chapter 12) would enter a negotiation looking for the I-win deal. When you ask them if they want a win–win agreement, of course they're going to say yes. That's a very powerful defense.

> "We agreed from the start that we would search for options that benefit everybody because that's the only way to have a successful long-term relationship—which we also agreed was important to us.
> I'm sure that if we keep working we can find a solution that's good for both you and me."

For the other side to disagree, they must admit that they are looking to get a one-sided, unfair pact. Most people don't want that, and if they do, they won't want to admit it. The bottom line is that you'll wind up with an agreement that you can all live with. One caveat: make sure that what you're pushing for is fair.

The Standard of Fairness

A negotiated agreement is fair when you would accept it, no matter which side you are on. This, of course, is when you are thinking from their perspective, not your own. (Otherwise you could fall into the "It's good enough for me, so it's good enough for them" trap.)

> When on business, Bruce always rents a large car because he feels they are safer. To cut costs, he makes his employees rent economy cars. Bruce isn't being fair because he won't accept his own rules.

Bringing Out Concerns

During the negotiation, you want to answer as many concerns as you can. You also want to put on the table all your concerns. If people aren't committing, it's because they still have concerns that need to be taken care of. You discover these concerns simply by asking—with persever-ance you'll get the particulars that you need.

Ask Open-Ended Questions—Give Complete Answers

Open-ended questions are questions that can't be answered in one word, like "yes" or "no." Open-ended questions call for a more complete answer and should be used when gathering information. Don't ask some-one, "Did you get my proposal?" Instead, say "What did you think of my proposal?" This will lead to a more forthcoming and valuable response.

Even if people gathering information ask you questions that can be answered in one word, make sure that you give them a more complete answer.

> **RALPH:** Did you get my proposal?
> **HELEN:** Yes, I did. I liked it, and I had a few questions about your cash flow projections. . . .

Use Closed-Ended Questions for Clear Response

Closed-ended questions are those that can be answered in only one word, usually "yes" or "no." They are effective when used to glean very specific responses that leave no murky areas about what one is thinking. For instance, "Do you want to use the slide projector?" When you get your response, you know precisely that person's plans are for the pro-jector. The beauty of a closed-ended question is that you'll get clear feedback of one sort or another.

When you're asking how people feel about your ideas, positive input is great. Unfavorable responses are helpful, too, because they carry with them important clues you need to develop a win–win deal. Only ask one closed-ended question at a time, especially to Introverts who will be processing each question separately. Avoid, "What do you think? Any-thing else? Do we have a deal?", before you get an answer. The re-sponse you get could be to your first, second, third, or all three queries.

Testing the Waters

Have you ever noticed that there are two kinds of people in the world? One type goes into water slowly, acclimating their body to the changing environment, while the other just plunges in. The first type tests the waters before committing their heads.

Testing the waters is a great technique for negotiators, too. Instead of asking if someone likes an entire package, ask them what parts they like and don't like. Nobody wants to hear you blurt out, "What's the hold-up?" Instead, gauge reactions to proposals by asking subtle, non-threatening questions. After you have a series of positive responses, you'll know you're close to an agreement.

Salespeople constantly test the waters with customers so that they can predict when is a good time to ask someone to take their checkbook out. They know that if they ask too soon, potential customers will think they're pushy; and if they wait too long to ask, they won't even get a shot at it. For example, let's say you're buying a coat. Let's also say you're concerned with three things: the color, the warmth, and the price. If the salesperson asks you if you like the coat, and there's one aspect that doesn't meet your criteria, more often than not you'll just say you don't like the coat and not go into details.

By testing the waters, the salesperson tries to figure out what exactly about the coat you like and don't like. The goal is to find you a coat that has everything you want, and nothing you don't want:

> **SALESPERSON:** What do you think of the color? (Information gathering.)
> **CUSTOMER:** I like it. I can wear it with other outfits, and it won't go out of style.
> **SALESPERSON:** Do you have a price range? (Response seeking.)
> **CUSTOMER:** Yes, and this coat is in my price range.
> **SALESPERSON:** Do you have any other concerns? (Testing the waters.)
> **CUSTOMER:** Yes. It's too heavy for most of the year.
> **SALESPERSON:** The lining is removable. Here, let me show you. (Concern handling.)

Begin Assessing Their Concerns

Testing the waters is a soft or easy attempt to reach closure in a sale or a negotiation. Testing the waters is a soft close because, like real water, all you're doing is dipping your toe in to get the temperature. Here's how it works: you ask very subtly if they are ready to make a commitment. You usually won't get a commitment because it's very early in the process, and the other side may still be developing questions or concerns. Occasionally, people will surprise you by saying "yes" before you think they're ready. Testing the waters lets you find out, in a non-threatening manner, "where they are" and "where you are."

Assess Their Response to Your Concerns

Put out a few of your ideas to the issues being negotiated. Gauge their reaction. If their reaction says, "Try something different" or "I'm not convinced," move on.

Step 1: Begin Testing the Waters

"We could begin the project next month." Negative reaction: "Hold on. We don't know which department's getting the project." Positive reaction: "When next month?"

"I'll need to place an ad to hire more salespeople." Negative reaction: "I wouldn't do that until we are sure you're going to be our Southern distributor." Positive reaction: "Good, that way we can get started right away."

Step 2: Measure Their Reaction

Sometimes you'll get a non-verbal reaction instead of a verbal response. Look for it. The appearance of being physically or emotionally taken aback, a sigh, grunt, or other displeasing sound, even pained looks—all are signs that there's something wrong.

Step 3: Float the Trial Balloon

Testing the waters sets up the trial balloon. The trial balloon is another "soft" close that sometimes gets a commitment, but its primary purpose is to bring concerns to the table. The reason that you sometimes wrap up a deal now is that you hear, "It sounds good to me" and "Let's do it" before you realize they're ready.

For the trial balloon, you want to take control, and keep the conversation on track. They may be so intent on telling you about their golf game or weekend plans, they never get around to saying, "It's okay by me."

Here, use closed-ended questions, with one-word answers, to get specific answers to specific questions. This is the opposite of the tactic used in the information-gathering stage when you want others to tell you as much as they can. One-word answers leave you in control because you can more easily direct the conversation if you're doing the talking. Here are some examples:

"Have I addressed all your concerns?"
"Do you have any other questions?"

If the answer to either one of these questions is "yes," proceed to the wrapping-up stage (covered in chapter 6). If you have a commitment, shake hands or write it up, depending how formal the negotiation is. If the answer is "no," then go to handling concerns, information gathering, or continue negotiating, depending on the situation.

Go back to information gathering if there's still some critical piece of information that needs to be figured into the equation. You address concerns when there's something that's unclear or unacceptable about a proposal. You negotiate when more alternatives need to be uncovered, or you need to change direction altogether.

Put Yourself in Their Shoes

A good way to anticipate concerns it to "walk in their shoes for a while." What things would be important to you if you were them? Be them instead of you for a moment. When you'd deal with you, you're ready to deal with them. What are the things people want? Here's a short list:

1. honesty in dealing
2. people who know what they're talking about
3. straightforward answers
4. win–win solutions
5. lasting relationships

What's missing? Smoothness, being a captivating speaker, having a flowing vocabulary. The ability to express yourself well is always in your favor, but you don't need to be a skilled orator to be an outstanding negotiator. Providing the five "basics" above will ensure that your negotiations will be fruitful and that people will respect you.

Remember that you're not just the deal seller, you're also the deal accepter. Here's how to manage that role.

When You Say Yea or Nay

Negotiations put you in the unique position of simultaneously making and receiving proposals. Again, your personality type determines how you react to other's offers. Generally speaking, you can have three reactions to another's suggestion to you: hot, lukewarm, and cold. Specifically speaking, you can experience a panoply of emotions that are variations on these themes. By knowing your own personality type, and the personality types of the parties you're negotiating with, you can see to it that your concerns are dealt with properly. The most important thing to remember is to always give a reason why you're rejecting an idea.

Always Give a Reason

By explaining your reasons for rejecting a proposal made by someone else, you've made enormous strides toward preserving or enhancing a relationship. If someone goes through the effort to make a proposal, and it is categorically rejected, the rejectee is likely to feel that both the idea and the idea-creator are not valued. Any negotiator who rejects a proposal without an explanation runs the risk of being perceived as difficult, unreasonable, and not listening. Of all the things that people hate in the world, not being listened to or taken seriously are absolutely at the top of the list.

It may be that the person quick to reject *is* listening, *likes* the idea, but just thinks the idea is unworkable. However, that's not likely to be the perception, and in many negotiations favorable perception is the key to success.

And the Reason Is

The other side doesn't have to like your justifications, or even agree with what you say. But if what you tell them is framed in terms of their personality type, you'll find that what they'll hear is, "I don't agree with you, but let's continue talking." Let's look now at how people want and don't want others' concerns explained to them.

How to Address Thinking-Type Concerns

Reinforce the logic in their suggestion, and say that your balking doesn't mean the idea doesn't make sense, but that it is just not taking enough of the variables into account. Then fill in the missing data. Let's look at an example.

> **DON:** We should have all our people send their faxes to the West Coast after 5:00 to get the lower phone rates. This way we could save money and the branch office will get their documents by 2:30 their time.

What *not* to say:

ANDREA: No. That won't work.

After this exchange, Don, a Thinking type, senses that his ideas are not highly regarded. Don spent time analyzing the fax usage and came up with this plan to save money. Now Don feels his ideas are not being considered, he's not appreciated, and he'll be reluctant to voice money-saving suggestions in the future, because he'll fear similar treatment.

What *to* say:

ANDREA: That is a good idea, Don, and sometimes we can do that. On the other hand, during lunch, the branch manager likes to discuss the requests we send, which means that sending faxes after 5:00 would be too late.

This time Don hears that his idea was considered, but learns that there are essential facts (lunchtime conversations) that he was unaware of. Don feels valued and listened to, and will keep cost-saving plans churning.

Not Having All the Data Is Common

When policies come raining down like manna from heaven, it is the rule, rather than the exception, that much thought went into making the policy or guideline. However, it's equally common for the people on the receiving end to get only the edict without the thought process that went into the creation of the rule. After someone hears the rationale, they may still disagree with the policy, but they don't feel personally infringed upon.

Once again, it's a way of separating the person from the problem. With reasons, the issue is the problem; without reasons, the issue is the person.

Negotiating with Feeling Types

Feeling types tend to merge their self-concept, ideas, and actions together, while Thinking types can dissociate actions with their self-concept. For instance, if a Thinking type suggested pepperoni pizza for an office party and some people voiced their displeasure in pepperoni, Thinking types would tend to think, "They don't like pepperoni," and reason that no matter how hard you try, you can't please everyone.

Feeling types, especially the more extreme Feeling types, upon hearing the complaints would think, "They don't like the pizza I picked out, so that means they don't like me." Also, the disharmony created by the pepperoni haters would be too unpleasant for the Feeling type to bear.

Thinking types need to add consideration of people's emotions to their analysis, and Feeling types need to try to dissociate when they're dealing with a neutral subject. Still, when speaking with Feeling types, be aware of people and their emotions in your response.

> **CARL:** I think it would be fun if the entire department went away for a ski weekend. That way we could all get to know each other personally as well as professionally.

What *not* to say:

> **RACHEL:** I'm afraid that just won't work.

What Carl hears is that his idea is inferior, and he is inferior for thinking of it. He probably feels that Rachel is cold-hearted and that she thinks intra-office harmony is unimportant. Carl, who has a knack for coming up with good ideas to boost morale, will be reluctant to bring out future ideas. Since Carl is a Feeling type, Rachel should avoid the cost/benefit/budget-type arguments that would work with a Thinking type, and focus her statements on the human/emotional unfeasibility she feels about the idea.

What *to* say:

> **RACHEL:** I know that the people in the department are all sociable and friendly, and doing something together is a great idea. I think some would feel uncomfortable being thrown together socially for such a long time. If you can think of something a little less time-intensive, let me know.

Here, Carl hears that Rachel doesn't think the ski-weekend idea is workable, but she wants to hear others.

Intuitive Feeling Types

A special mention here needs to be made regarding Intuitive Feeling types. These types are outstanding at coming up with ideas that take into consideration all of the possible feelings people may have on any given subject. They always seem to have their antennas tuned to the myriad of feelings around them. With each feeling they pick up comes an analysis of its possible meanings. You're wise to consult an Intuitive Feeling Type during any emotionally charged negotiation.

Wrapping Things Up

After you understand the concerns of the people sitting proverbially across the table from you, and they understand yours, the next step is to finish things up and get a commitment. That's covered next chapter.

Conclusion

Concerns are reasons you or the people you're negotiating with have for *not* wanting to make a commitment. Each concern needs to be addressed before moving to the final stage of the negotiation—wrapping it up. After asking and answering questions designed to learn about what's important to both sides, follow these steps:

STEP 1: Begin testing the waters.
STEP 2: Measure their responses.
STEP 3: Float the trial balloon.

You can expect different types of objections from Thinking and Feeling types. Thinking types base decisions on analytical reasoning, while Feeling types base decisions on personal values and improving harmony. Thinking types aren't smarter than Feeling types, nor are their decisions better, just reasoned and impersonal.

Thinking	Feeling
Decides based on reason.	Decides based on personal values.
Thinks of groups impersonally.	Thinks of groups as individuals.

Make sure all of your and their concerns are ameliorated before attempting to wrap things up.

NOTE

1. Myers and McCaulley, *Manual: A Guide to MBTI*, 248–250.

Chapter 6
COMING TO AGREEMENT

Chapter 3 looked at how people interact socially. Chapter 4 covered how people want information presented to them, and chapter 5 examined how to address concerns. This chapter looks at how to seal the deal.

Wrapping up a deal is the most difficult part of negotiation for many people. With Personality Negotiating, getting a commitment proceeds easily and smoothly because you'll know beforehand how people react to closure. There are two personality factors in the closing equation: personality type and conflict-resolution style. We'll look at both.

Up to now, assume that both parties are communicating, they understand each other, and they've responded positively to each other's trial balloons. Furthermore, together they have forged a deal that will have both sides come out winners. All the hard work is about to pay off! Getting together on an agreement will be easy, since *both sides* will walk away with a deal destined to benefit all.

One Caveat

There is one caveat. People have different senses of time. They look at closure, or the sense that an agreement has been reached, differently. Knowing how to effectively manage closure is the key to getting a commitment to a final agreement.

The fourth Personality Negotiating preference, the Judging/Perceiving index, is the first key to managing closure. We'll look at that next.

The Judging/Perceiving Index

Judging and Perceiving types view time very differently. Judging types have a concrete sense of time and like making plans and schedules and adhering to them. When faced with a decision, they seek closure.

Perceiving types have a general concept of time and like minimal schedules; they dislike deadlines or closure, preferring to keep their options open.

Judging types tend to have appointment books while Perceiving types tend to stick notes up around the office. (Intuitive Judging appointment books have each month on a page and only contain major events, while

Sensing Judging appointment books tend to have a separate page for each day so there is more room to write.)

When Judging types plan to do something by Friday, they'll complete the task by then, because that was the plan. Perceiving types wait until they're sure they're doing the right thing and the fact that it's Friday or any other day is irrelevant.

When you negotiate with Judging types, set up a deadline schedule with them. They'll usually keep to it. When you negotiate with Perceiving types, find out what they need to know, what problems need to be solved, and the sequence of events that need to take place before they'll act. If they're reluctant to commit on a direction to take, reinforce the benefits or necessity of finally deciding.

The Judging/Perceiving preference, in combination with the Introvert/Extrovert preference, also determines the person's "dominant function." For instance, the ESTJ (Extrovert, Sensing, Thinking, *Judging*) type has a dominant, or favorite, function of Thinking, from the third preference index. The ESTP (Extrovert, Sensing, Thinking, *Perceiving*) type has a dominant, or favorite, function of Sensing, from the second preference index. This will be covered in detail in chapter 8.

If you're interested in finding out now if you are a Judging or Perceiving type, respond to the following statements:

DIRECTIONS: Read each of these items and circle answer A or B, depending on which response fits you best. There aren't any right, wrong, or better answers. You'll find the key to scoring at the end of the test.

1. **You tend to like days that are:**
   A) spontaneous.
   B) tightly scheduled.
2. **When you make a significant decision, you usually:**
   A) allot yourself time to make it.
   B) take as much time as you need.
3. **When you make major purchases, they are usually:**
   A) unplanned.
   B) planned.
4. **If you made a bad decision, you would feel:**
   A) it was the best decision at the time.
   B) you were rushed.
5. **If you're given a deadline for making a decision, and there's not enough time, you would:**
   A) allow the deadline to slip until you have all the data.
   B) make it anyway, with the data you do have.

6. **You've just made a major decision. You are most likely:**
   A) relieved the decision is over.
   B) worried that your decision wasn't right.
7. **If you overloaded your appointment schedule one day, you would:**
   A) try to reschedule some appointments.
   B) try to keep all the appointments, even if it is difficult.
8. **You think it's important to have a:**
   A) concrete sense of time.
   B) general sense of time.
9. **You're usually:**
   A) late.
   B) on time.
10. **When you buy something with several options:**
    A) you decide when you are comfortable that you have enough information.
    B) you set up a deadline for making a final decision, and then work to get all the information by that deadline.
11. **If you came to a fork in the woods, you would take:**
    A) the road less travelled.
    B) the road more travelled.

SCORING:
Add the **A** answers for questions
2, 4, 6, 8
Add the **B** answers for questions
1, 3, 5, 7, 9, 10, 11

Put the Total here:_____ **J/P**

If the Total is 6 or more you're most likely a **Judging** type. Otherwise, you're most likely a **Perceiving** type.

Occupations Common to Judging and Perceiving Types

Here's a list of professions and occupations commonly chosen by Judging and Perceiving types.[1]

Judging Types Predominate	Perceiving Types Predominate
chemical engineer	journalist
nurse	surveyor
sales manager	editor

judge	carpenter
dentist	actor
steel worker	psychologist
banker	athlete
physician	restaurant worker
teacher	research assistant
manager	writer and entertainer

Judging types are likely to object that finalizing an agreement is taking too long. Perceiving types will object to being rushed into a decision.

How to Recognize Judging or Perceiving Types

You know when someone is a Judging or Perceiving type by the kind of responses he or she gives to questions about time, schedules, and closure. As reported above, Judging types seek closure and try to make definitive schedules and to honor them. Perceiving types avoid making schedules and setting deadlines and delay closure until they're certain the decision they're making is a good one. Here are some examples with Tom, a Judging type in Marketing, and Ann Marie, a Perceiving type in the R&D department.

Tom's responsibilities include making sure that software products like TrueSoft, a package that checks for spreadsheet errors, gets out on schedule, while Ann Marie's job is to guarantee that TrueSoft is bug-free. Today is Wednesday. After three previous delays, TrueSoft is again scheduled for release on Friday. Ann Marie's department hasn't finished the Quality Assurance (QA) test yet and she won't sign off on the software so that it can be copied and shipped.

> **TOM:** Our customers are very eager to get their shipments of TrueSoft. We already have over 500 back orders, and the salespeople say that unless we ship Friday for delivery by Monday, we'll have a slew of purchase orders cancelled. Even if there are a few bugs, we need your department's approval today to have time to prepare and ship the software out as is, or lose lots of money.

Tom's Judging type concerns are characterized by firm deadlines (needing the software shipped by Friday), closure (a decision must be made today), and a firm sense of the timing involved in the steps needed to complete the task by the end of the week (knowing it takes two days for packaging and shipping).

ANN MARIE: The software still isn't perfect, and I don't want to send out anything that is sub par. I'll sign off on the software release when I'm sure that it's ready. We're working very hard on it, but I can't give you a completion date. TrueSoft will be ready when the software runs in its entirety without problems—and we don't know when that will happen until it does.

Ann Marie's Perceiving type answer is characterized by an *event deadline*, not a time deadline. (I'll sign off . . . when the software runs . . . without problems"—which is important.) Although there have already been three delays, she won't give her approval until she's satisfied. If the software is proven bug-free in an hour, she'll act in an hour. If the substantiation she needs comes next year, she'll approve the software for shipment next year.

Quick vs. Careful Decision Making

Judging types, like Tom, tend to make decisions quickly. If Tom has his way, delivery dates will always be met, although customer satisfaction will be low and support costs will be high because of bugs in the software that Ann Marie's team didn't have time to catch.

Perceiving types, like Ann Marie, tend to make big decisions more slowly. The software Ann Marie approves always works perfectly, but if the sales cycle drags on too long, Ann Marie's company could lose money because they can't ship. (Computer magazines call promised, but undelivered software "vaporware!")

Discover Perceiving Type's Event Schedule

Remember, Ann Marie is being truthful when she says that she'll okay the software for shipment when TrueSoft is bug-free. A Perceiving-type's event schedule is usually well thought-out. Anyway, it will be a significant matter to them, so don't try to shrug it off with, "Don't worry about that. It's good enough," and leave it at that. Ask her, instead,

TOM: I understand your concern. However, we feel that the software is functional. Is it?
ANN MARIE: Yes, it's functional, but there are still some parts of the interface that are unclear. I feel that people will have trouble using it.

You'll find negotiating with Perceiving Types much easier if you ask them what their concerns are, how strongly they feel about the concern, how you can handle the concern, and, most especially, what event schedule needs to be satisfied to get a commitment.

Keep to Judging Type's Schedule

If Judging types, like Tom, ask you to get back to them by Friday, make sure you do it. Keeping to Judging-types' schedules will garner you their support, while delaying their schedules will annoy them. Judging types tend to make schedules for everything, but they won't always explicitly tell you what their schedules are unless prompted (especially Introverted Judging types). To find out, just ask them.

The Wrapping-Up Process in Action

Here's an example of how a negotiation wrap-up works. Tom and Ann Marie are at odds because of conflicting roles and personality types. However, let's see how they do using Personality Negotiating.

Step 1: Review What's Important

First, review everyone's decision criteria. Look to your notes or use your recall to explain the concerns and objections that are on the table.

> **TOM:** As head of quality control, it is important to you that the products we sell are bug-free and work perfectly. Right?
> **ANN MARIE:** Not really. They don't have to work perfectly, but they do need to be usable. I'm worried that TrueSoft, in its current state, could be unusable as a commercial product.
> **TOM:** So, your primary concern is that TrueSoft be usable.
> **ANN MARIE:** Yes. And when I'm assured it is, I'll okay it. What's important to you?
> **TOM:** I don't want to lose any sales because we miss our delivery dates. Although some customers are willing to wait for TrueSoft to be completely bug-free, most of them are willing to take it as is, and wait for updates to perfect it.

Step 2: Find Out If Your Idea Fits Their Criteria

> **TOM:** How about if we ship out the product as is, announcing it as a beta version, and letting our customers know that it is still in QA? If we do this, they can get TrueSoft delivered to help them right away, and can get the final version later.

Then ask this:

> "Do you have any questions or concerns about what I've proposed?"

Asking the people you're negotiating with if they have any questions or concerns is a pleasant way of asking them if they have any problems with your proposal. Address concerns until both sides are happy with the outcome or can live with the specific components that are not optimal for them.

You've just about closed the deal! If you've met their concerns and they've met your concerns, ninety-nine percent of the time, you're done. Use closed-ended questions and use your knowledge of their personality temperament to gauge how much mustard to put behind your queries. Here are some samples to adapt to your situation.

Step 3: Ask for the Commitment

"Is this deal right for you?"
"Do we have a deal?"
"What's left to discuss?"
"What do you think?"
"What's the next step?"
"Should we schedule implementation?"
"Can I count on your support?"

Ask one wrap-up question at a time. And wait for the reply, remembering that Introverts need at least ten seconds to internalize a response. Extroverts may need some time, too, especially for significant decisions. Your job up to this point has been to discover common needs and to invent options. Assuming you're both winning, you should walk away happy. That's because unless either party is trying to scam or bully the other, both will walk away from the deal better off than before the bargaining began.

Step 4: Get It Down on Paper or Go Back to Handling Concerns

Sometimes objections don't become apparent until someone truly realizes the impact of their imminent decision. Sometimes it's only then that it's realized how much the budget will be hit, or how short-staffed the department will be. In most real-world situations you'll then have to retrace information gathering, handling concerns, trial closing, and attempted closing a few times before you seal the deal. Real-world negotiations might look like this:

1. Have an initial meeting
2. Gather information
3. Make the presentation

4. Attend a presentation
5. Handle concerns/generate concern list
6. Trial close
7. Have another presentation
8. Trial close
9. Handle concerns
10. Attempt close
11. Handle concerns
12. Trial close
13. Close
14. Finalize the deal

Your job is to keep things on track and moving smoothly. Having to repeat steps is not only normal, it's expected. Don't think that because the first idea wasn't accepted something is wrong. Think of the times when you were brainstorming and your first ideas, that seemed so promising, were later eclipsed by superior plans.

Keep Things Moving

After completing each step in the process, persevere until you're done. How much pressure do you use? That depends on the personality type of the people you're dealing with. It also depends on their conflict-resolution style, which we'll tackle soon. Before getting into that, there's a phenomenon that sometimes occurs soon after a deal is complete—wet feet. Technically, wet-feet syndrome is caused by lingering concerns. It can be frustrating, but needn't ruin your day.

Step 5: Addressing Lingering Concerns

Sometimes people come to a deal, but have a few reservations called "lingering concerns." Lingering concerns are usually small problems, but they can delay or halt a negotiation. The way you tie up these loose ends is to ask, "If I took care of (whatever the lingering concern is) would you feel comfortable deciding right now?" If the answer is yes, then the concession you gave just won you the deal. If the answer is no, then there's more to the lingering concern than meets the eye. Here, you'll need to go back to information gathering (covered in chapter 4).

Usually, giving a minor concession is worth it to prevent the agreement from falling through. If you don't close the deal now, you might never close it, or the negotiations could drag on forever.

Here's how to handle the lingering concerns of someone who is almost ready to commit:

BROKER: Do you have any final questions or concerns?
CUSTOMER: I like the house, but there's something about it that bothers me. (This is most likely the Sensing-type objection.)

INFORMATION GATHERING

BROKER: Is there anything else you want in a house that you don't see here?
CUSTOMER: No.

CONCERN HANDLING

BROKER: Is the price too high?
CUSTOMER: No, not really.

EXPLORING OPTIONS

BROKER: If you could change one thing, what would it be?
CUSTOMER: The owner had pets, and I'm worried that after I move in I'll find that the carpets are dirty and smelly.

The concern to focus on is the issue of the carpets. The broker knows that getting the carpets professionally cleaned will add $300 to the cost of the $100,000 condo.

BROKER: Let's write up an offer with a contingency that the seller has to pay to have the carpets professionally cleaned with a cleaner that offers a guarantee.
CUSTOMER: Okay.

Go back to step 1: Review their buying criteria.

BROKER: Is there anything else you wanted that I haven't covered?
CUSTOMER: No.

Go back to step 2: Find out if the new solution fits their buying criteria.

BROKER: Do you have any other questions or concerns?
CUSTOMER: No.

Go back to step 3: Ask for a commitment.

BROKER: Should we write it up right now?
CUSTOMER: Yes.
BROKER: Great!

Giving this concession was key to the buyer, who gets the carpets cleaned, but trivial to the seller eager to sell her house. If the broker didn't ask the buyer what specifically was the matter, the buyer may not have completed the thought process and would have only known she felt uneasy. If you finish the negotiation with lingering concerns dangling, a lingering concern could fester, and the deal could be lost.

What If Lingering Concerns Aren't Straightforward

Sometimes addressing lingering concerns takes more than getting the carpets cleaned. If handling difficult lingering concerns looks like it's going to take a while, make sure you have a commitment and work to wrap up the loose ends. Depending on the complexity of the negotiation and what's at stake, you may want to get a performance guarantee or letter of intent that spells out what's what.

> **FRED:** Before going into partnership with you, I'd want to have an independent party audit the financial statements. That's the only way I'd be sure, but to get a CPA involved would be expensive.
>
> **JULIE:** Is that the only concern you have, that's delaying you from becoming a partner?
>
> **FRED:** Yes.
>
> **JULIE:** An audit of the records isn't as expensive as you think. If you choose the accountant, I'll pick up the tab. Before I do that, I'll need an agreement that you'll go through with the investment assuming the books are in order.
>
> **JULIE:** That's fair.

Explain your needs on an adult–adult level, and the vast majority will understand you're being reasonable and be compliant. People know that there's no such thing as a free lunch and will be willing to acquiesce to many different strategies to get an agreement completed.

Crunchtime's Hidden Concerns

Sometimes crunchtime will bring out new concerns. Little things that are nagging at the other side, like:

> "This is an awfully big commitment."
> "I'm not sure I'm doing the right thing."
> "I just want to check a few more things."
> "I don't feel comfortable buying the first house I see."

When these last-minute hidden concerns surface, your frustration level can be unbearable. There's a tendency to want to force or guilt-trip people into agreement, which doesn't work, but does create bad feelings on everyone's part. Sometimes people just need reassurance,

"We've worked hard on this deal, and you need to believe we've covered every contingency."
In other cases, maybe all that is needed is some time:

"Before we look at any more proposals, let's take a couple of days to think about the decision we came to today. We were very careful but let's see if we missed anything." (The concern here isn't the decision, but the worry that some important decision criteria might have been missed. A few extra days gives the person time to ameliorate or set aside the concern.)

Generally people with hidden concerns will still come to an agreement with you, although the deal won't always resemble the one you thought you agreed to and the timing of the implementation may be later than you'd like.

Conflict-Resolution Style

The other part of behavior that you need to know when you're closing a deal is the conflict-resolution style of the people you're dealing with as well as your own. Fisher and Ury in *Getting to Yes* broke conflict-resolution style into two categories, hard and soft. Since then, others, including Robert Benfari, Ph.D. in *Understanding Your Management Style*,[2] have divided conflict-resolution into five categories:

Collaborative
Compromise
Win–Lose
Yield–Lose
Lose–Lose

Compromise and win–lose are hard styles (one tries to coerce another): yield–lose and lose–lose are soft styles (one allows himself or herself to be coerced). It is the collaborative style that eventually leads to a Win–Win outcome. According to conflict-resolution theory, people use all five styles at different times and in different situations.

For instance, if you're negotiating with your neighbor about how often your lawn should be mowed, you might start with a collaborative-negotiation stance. If one day you come home and the sheriff hands you a summons because your neighbor is suing you, you might bag the collaborative stance and seek to win the suit, and even countersue for their dog dooing on your lawn. (A worthy row for Judge Wapner's "People's Court.")

After the trials are over you may keep your lawn messy, although you don't like it very much, just to get the neighbor teed off at you (lose–lose). Finally, you may wish to avoid them whenever you can (yield–lose).

Observe yourself when you are faced with conflict. If you tend to quickly break the conflict down into what your needs are and seek a single answer that will fit your needs, then you have a hard primary conflict-resolution style.

If you tend to reach deals too quickly, or find yourself giving in and trying to preserve the relationship, then you have a soft primary conflict-resolution style.

If you're trying to assess both your concerns and their concerns, and work jointly to find collaborative solutions based on the concerns of the participants, you have a collaborative primary conflict-resolution style.

All People Have All Styles

Remember, all people have all styles. Your and their primary style is how you start resolving conflict, but not necessarily how you end conflict. If the person you're dealing with first insists on a lopsided (win–lose) deal, relentlessly give reasons why you won't accept the deal. Eventually they'll give up trying to dominate you and slip into their next style.

Their next style could be any one of the four remaining ones. If it's compromise, they'll try to sell you on the idea that half a pie is better than no pie—that may be true, but quite often you don't need to settle on a compromise—so keep struggling. Once again, if you persist in giving reasons why a collaborative deal is better than a compromise, they'll slip into their next style.

If their next style is collaborative (win–win), great. Work with them to invent options to secure a superior deal.

If their next style is yield–lose or lose–lose you're likely to hear things like, "Let's just forget the whole thing," or "This won't work." They may also physically yield by avoiding you.

Don't let this stage throw you. Remember that it's a stage and respond with encouragement and optimism: "If we forget about the whole thing, we'll both be losing. It will work. Let's look at more options."

Enthusiasm's contagious, and you'll find that your confidence in your collective ability to reach a deal will be a self-fulfilling prophesy.

After people start collaborative problem solving they are often struck by two points: 1) collaborative solutions can be the norm, and 2) collaborative solutions usually aren't complex.

Collaborative Solutions Can Be the Norm

Many people spend most of their lives resolving conflicts with their primary conflict-resolution style, which is often not win–win. This means they spend their time proposing one-sided deals, continuously compromising, or avoiding conflicts whenever they can.

It's quite a relief when they find that, with a little extra effort and observation on their parts, they can reach deals that are more satisfying for everyone.

Invent Options

Have you ever noticed that sometimes you delayed doing something, even though it seemed like it was the perfect answer, and were later glad you had held off because there was a much better way of doing it? Sometimes our first blush solution to a problem is the best . . . often it's not. If you've reached a stone wall and are having trouble inventing options, follow these five steps:

STEP 1: IDENTIFY What are the concerns? Finding out what's fueling concerns is the first big step in the invention process.

This sounds like it should be the easiest step of all, but without Personality Negotiating it's often the most time consuming and arduous one. Why? Because people are busy inventing options in a way that benefits them and they forget how it impacts all around and how others involved might see things or go about things differently. These last four chapters, on personality type, help both parties immeasurably at this stage.

Look into the symptoms and contrast them with "how things should be."

STEP 2: ANALYZE Figure out the problem. Here, you need to categorize the symptoms and discover, together, the pluses and minuses to each with suggested alternatives. Find out what's lacking and note the barriers to solutions.

STEP 3: STRATEGIZE Come up with ideas. You know what the barriers are, now you need to invent options to the barriers. Don't get too specific at this point, stick to generalizations.

STEP 4: OPERATIONALIZE What needs to happen to turn an idea into a plan? Now's the time to get specific. If you were to go down a certain path, what would it take? Do you have the resources, energy, budget, manpower, knowledge, experience, etc., to make the idea work? If not, where could you get the missing pieces?

Don't be too quick to cast away promising strategies because they seem, at first, too difficult. Many times, negotiations bog down because people jump to step five, rating the ideas, too quickly and discard options as useless or unfeasible. Thomas Edison said that genius is one percent inspiration and ninety-nine percent perspiration. He was right. I hate to break it to some of you, but there is no substitute for working hard at this stage.

STEP 5: QUANTIFY Rate the ideas. List all of the options you've invented and rank them according to what you feel are their probabilities of success. When you're all done, choose *together* which has the best chance of succeeding and go with it.

Collaborative Solutions Aren't Rocket Science

The second Personality Negotiating surprise to people is the fact that coming up with a solution that fits everyone's concern often isn't all that difficult. In fact, it's rare that a compatible solution *can't* be found. After a while you'll get so proficient at inventing options that some of the steps will meld. This is happening because there's a flurry of activity going on in the negotiators' brains. As long as you're not going so fast that you become frustrated or careless, have fun. Here's an example of a real-life case that's typical of the kind of resolutions good negotiators can invent together:

STEP 1: What's the concern?

> Emergimed is a fifty hospital chain that uses Medi-Pay's software in the emergency department computers for billing. Delta Laboratories has software that they want to sell to Emergimed, but Emergimed says that they won't buy until they're sure Delta Labs' system is compatible with Medi-Pay's.

After some months of unsuccessfully trying to get their software to work with Medi-Pay, so that the text properly fits the computer screen, Delta Labs is ready to throw in the towel and forfeit the $500,000 that the fifty sales would bring them.

STEP 2: Analyze the problem.

Although the technical expertise that Emergimed, Medi-Pay, and Delta Labs have might well be able to solve the fit problem, Delta Labs' management feels that the long shot is not worth the cost involved in flying the technical and marketing teams to a central location.

STEPS 3, 4, and 5: Plan strategy, get specific, and rate the ideas.

Top idea: having several people simultaneously looking at a computer screen and talking, but bringing all the people together is too expensive, a barrier. Test barrier: What if some people got together? Barrier: Still too expensive.

Test barrier: How about a conference call? Barrier: The issue is too complex for a conference call.

The only cost of testing the barrier is a few minutes' time and a small amount of money. With little to lose, it was agreed to give it a try.

What was done

THE SOLUTION: Have a conference call involving the marketing and technical staffs of the three organizations.
THE OUTCOME: The conference call took twenty minutes. It turned out that the problem was an inadvertent tab statement left in the program by one of Delta's programmers. The problem was quickly identified and fixed, the software worked, and Emergimed bought Delta Labs' system for each of their fifty hospitals.

As you can see, the final strategy was simple. Negotiators are usually astounded at how easy solutions can be when everyone pitches in. More involved case studies are coming up in the next chapter.

Conclusion

After the presentation, ask for questions, handle concerns, trial close, negotiate, and wrap up the deal. Every negotiation usually detours back to an earlier stage before concluding with an agreement.

When completing the deal, follow these five steps:

STEP 1: Review the criteria.
STEP 2: Find out if the invented solution fits your and their criteria.
STEP 3: Ask if they are ready to commit.
STEP 4: Shake hands or go back to handling concerns.
STEP 5: Handle lingering concerns (if necessary).

If you're having difficulty coming up with options, follow this procedure:

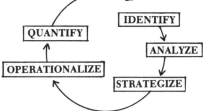

Remember that a necessary part of inventing is to not stifle creativity. Allow everyone time to come up with suggestions and express their original ideas.

Judging and Perceiving Types

Judging types have a concrete sense of time and think it's necessary to commit to a decision when deadlines arrive. Perceiving types have a more general concept of time and think it's important to decide carefully, taking as much time as they need. Perceiving types have an event schedule that needs to be satisfied before they'll commit.

Judging	Perceiving
Has a concrete sense of time.	Has a general concept of time.
Seeks closure in decisions.	Delays closure in decisions.
Likes things to be planned.	Likes things to be spontaneous.
Has a time schedule.	Has an event schedule.

How Judging and Perceiving Types Want to Be Presented To

JUDGING types want the presentation itself to be timely and efficient. The solution needs to fit into their time schedules.

PERCEIVING types will want to make good decisions. They'll allow you as much time as you need to present. Make sure you are as complete as possible, especially when relating to their "dominant function."

Coming to Agreement 93

Conflict Resolution

Conflict-resolution style is the series of responses made when confronting any disagreement. We start with our primary style and, if that doesn't work, go on to successive styles as the conflict progresses. For example, people who have the resolution style—Win–Lose, Compromise, Lose–Lose, Collaborative, and Yield–Lose—will solve conflicts this way:

> First they will try hard to "win" by strongly advocating their position. When they meet resistance, they will try to compromise. If compromise doesn't work and they meet more resistance, they may give up and walk away. After waiting a while, they'll come back and try to resolve the problem collaboratively. If that doesn't work, they'll accept any option, even one that doesn't benefit them.

Here's an easy way to remember the conflict-resolution styles:

Compromise: Split the pie

Lose–Lose: Destroy the pie

Win–Lose: Take the whole pie
(Lose–Win: Give up the whole pie)

Yield–Lose: Walk away
from the person, and the pie

Collaborative: Make two pies

Collaborative solutions are the norm when you try for them, and they are often not complex.

NOTES

1. Myers and McCaulley, *Manual: A Guide to MBTI*, 250–253.
2. Robert Benfari with Jean Knox, *Understanding Your Management Style: Beyond the Myers-Briggs Type Indicator* (Lexington, Mass.: Lexington Books, 1991), 40–48.

Chapter 7
PERSONALITY NEGOTIATING CASE STUDIES

Now that you have a good idea of how Personality Negotiating works from start to finish, here are three different case studies. The first is an in-depth look at a negotiation involving three employees trying to negotiate a change in company policy with the same ISTJ (*Introverted, Sensing, Thinking, Judging*) boss. The second is a peek at a typical Judging and Perceiving type vacation day. Third is a reader-participation exercise that gives you a chance to figure out the personality types of two different people.

Case Study I—How Personality Negotiating Works

This first case involves three branch managers of Hudson Plastics, each trying to negotiate a change in company policy with the district manager. One manager uses Personality Negotiating, while the others use other methods to try to sway the manager. Let's see how the branch managers, working for satellite offices of Hudson Plastics, tackle the same problem.

All are unhappy with Harry Drake's policy of insisting on: 1) a three-hour sales meeting at 6:30 each Monday morning, and 2) complex and time-consuming 30/60/90-day reports from each salesperson each week. Harry is the district manager for Hudson Plastics.

The branch managers are: Tracy, from the Boston office; Paul, from the Worcester office; and Alex, from the Hartford office. Their personality profiles are as follows:

ALEX (HARTFORD OFFICE): Alex is an ESTP (*Extroverted, Sensing, Thinking, Perceiving*) type. He will: 1) want to talk about his concerns (*Extrovert*); 2) go into a detailed proposal line by line (*Sensing*); 3) assume that if a proposal makes sense it will be accepted (this is how a Thinking type thinks); and 4) be driven by event, not time, schedules for completion (*Perceiving*). Alex does *not* Personality Negotiate.

PAUL (WORCESTER OFFICE): Paul is an ISFJ (*Introverted, Sensing, Feeling, Judging*) type. Paul, like other ISFJ's, will: 1) want to discuss proposals (Extrovert); 2) go into a detailed proposal line by line (Sensing); 3) wish that unpopular policies be revised or deleted (Feeling); and 4) want closure on a tight, predetermined schedule (Judging). Paul will *not* be Personality Negotiating.

TRACY (BOSTON OFFICE): Tracy is an ENFP (*E*xtroverted, *I*ntuitive, *F*eeling, *P*erceiving) type. Tracy's type is the opposite of Harry's, but she *will* Personality-Negotiate. 1) Tracy knows that her preference is to talk about solutions, but that she must let Introverts see her proposals before talking about them and let Introverts think after she asks them questions. 2) Because of Tracy's Intuitive nature, she'd rather delve into the theory of managing salespeople and have a brainstorming session trying to invent options first-off. Yet she knows that when she deals with Sensates that she must avoid theoretical arguments, and do the brainstorming ahead of time so that Harry only hears the most promising and practical idea. (She also knows that, as an Extrovert, she should talk the ideas through with someone before broaching the subject with Harry.) 3) Her Feeling function will motivate her to act because her sales team is getting cranky about their Monday "sunrise" meetings. She also sees them becoming agitated because they're torn between doing complete reports and falling behind in returning customers' phone calls. On the other hand, Tracy also values a harmonious relationship with her boss and often feels torn by the resentment and irritation being created on both sides. She knows that when dealing with Thinking types, like Harry, she must avoid emotionally based arguments and stick to analytical ones. 4) Finally, Tracy's Perceiving function tells her that she would prefer to have an event deadline drive her readiness to speak to Harry, but that she may have to look beyond her wishes. She would prefer being flexible about the reports and meeting times, but she knows that she must respect that Harry doesn't feel the same way.

Personality Profile of Harry

Harry is an ISTJ (*I*ntroverted, *S*ensing, *T*hinking, *J*udging) type. This means that: 1) Harry wants to see proposals and supporting data in a memo first, and dislikes hashing out the issues on the phone (Introvert), 2) he wants relevant facts and practical solutions (Sensing), 3) he wants arguments to be based on "clear thought," not on emotion (Thinking), and, 4) having his employees keep to his timetables is very important to him (Judging). (Another trait common to ISTJ types is that they tend to feel that hard work and sacrifice are expected of employees, so the fact that he's asking much of them isn't bothersome to him.)

What Are the Issues?

Let's look at the issues of this case from all sides.

ACCORDING TO HARRY: Harry took over as district manager six months ago. He used to travel to the different offices to get the statistics for compiling his monthly reports to senior management. He found these trips to be time-consuming and frustrating because the data was often late, or sloppily thrown together at the last minute.

Harry, who came from the financial side of the company, was irked to find many salespeople not arriving at work until 9:30 or 10:00 on Monday mornings. He felt that they were being paid a salary and they should be earning it. They explained that their customers don't get settled in until 9:30 or 10:00 anyway, and don't want salespeople calling so early.

Harry solved the problem of not getting the figures for his reports by insisting that he receive the information he needs regularly. He reasoned that the reports would take some time to do at first, but then become easier as time went on.

He also felt that the reps didn't always have up-to-date information and that more sales meetings were necessary. Since the reps had told him that Monday mornings before 10:00 were dead time anyway, that's when the meetings were scheduled.

Harry understands that the reps are griping, but he feels if they don't like it, they can quit. He knows attrition is high since the policy was instituted, but figures it'll level off in a few weeks.

ACCORDING TO THE BRANCH MANAGERS: The branch managers find Monday to be little more than a litany of complaints from the sales team. Not much gets done at the meetings, and they are sparsely attended. They find the reps working on the reports until after lunch, and all the reps claim to "have meetings" or have to "go cold calling" at around 2:00—when in reality they're calling it a day.

The managers find that Mondays, which used to be productive, are now pretty much a waste. Also, they're finding that reps that used to work overtime are now putting in the minimum time required. The worst part of it is that the 30/60/90-day customer-buying forecasts the reps do are fairly accurate in the 30-day range, but are wildly off-target three months down the road.

Finally, the managers are seeing their best reps quit, while the reps who are staying are their average or underperformers. And they, themselves, are spending more and more time answering rookie questions from the new hires instead of nursing high-volume accounts.

Telling Harry About Their Problems with the Policy

HOW ALEX APPROACHES HARRY: Alex, from the Hartford office, is the first to contact Harry. (Remember, Alex is an ESTP, and won't be Personality Negotiating.) On a whim, Alex drives to the corporate headquarters in Hudson, New Hampshire. When Alex arrives, he is very angry with Harry. Two of his best reps had handed in their resignations, citing having to get up at 5:00 A.M. and having Mondays squandered as the reasons behind their leaving.

Harry has been in meetings all day, but agrees to see Alex because of the effort that Alex has made in coming up to New Hampshire.

> **ALEX:** We've got to can these Monday morning meetings. I'm losing my very best people because of them, and you've got to make a change right away.

Harry, an Introvert, has just been in a series of meetings and hasn't had time to charge his batteries. He sees Alex's argument as passionate, but had included in his evaluation of the policy the likelihood that some good people would quit. Before instituting the new policy, Harry had come to the conclusion that the benefits of getting people to work bright and early were worth the cost of a few "lazy" people quitting.

> **HARRY:** Alex, I know you're upset, and I know that having some of your best people quit will bring some short-term wrinkles. But if they want to saunter into work any old time they'd like, then, frankly, I don't want them working for us. I know you'll get some good replacements. If you have any concerns, why not write them up in a memo, and I'll look at them the first chance I get.

Harry is, unknowingly, giving Alex a major clue to making his arguments strong: putting them in memo form and sending them to Harry to pore over privately. But Alex doesn't know about Personality Negotiating:

> **ALEX:** Forget it. You've heard everything I have to say.

Alex leaves for Hartford frustrated and concerned that he'll lose his entire sales force.

HOW PAUL TRIES: Paul is from the Worcester office. His ISFJ personality type is similar to, but not the same as Harry's. Since Paul, like Harry, is an Introverted, Sensing, Judging type, the way he presents, and its form, will mesh with Harry's style. Since Paul, however, is a

Feeling type and Harry's a Thinking type, and Paul is *not* Personality Negotiating, the content is way off.

Paul begins by writing a memo that focuses on how he and the reps feel about meeting so early, and how it's creating disharmony. After reading Paul's memo, Harry phones Paul. Harry empathizes with Paul's concerns, but tells him that his job is no picnic either:

> **HARRY:** I know it's tough on some reps, but if Monday morning meetings are hard for them, why don't they just go to sleep a little earlier? They don't have to do their reports on Mondays, either, they could work on them in the office over the weekend. That way they can get right to work after the meeting.
> **PAUL:** I don't think they're going to like those ideas very much.
> **HARRY:** They're making good money, and if they don't want to pay their dues, that's okay. I planned on some whining and a few people taking off. It will stabilize soon enough. You've got to keep them motivated and focused.

Finally Tracy, from the Boston office, will contact Harry.

HOW TRACY TRIES: Tracy, from the Boston office, phones Harry late Tuesday afternoon after his corporate meeting. Although this is normally a poor time to call Introverts like Harry, she uses Personality Negotiating to glean how and when to discuss important matters with him:

> **TRACY:** Good afternoon, Harry, this is Tracy. Is this a convenient time to call?
> **HARRY:** It's okay. I just got out of our corporate meeting. What's on your mind?

Tracy knows Harry is an Introvert who's probably feeling fatigued from the meeting, so she suggests an alternative:

> **TRACY:** I've got some things to discuss with you. Would you prefer that I put them down in a memo and fax them over to you, or would you like to discuss them now?
> **HARRY:** If you write up a memo, I can give it much more attention than if we discuss it.

She now knows Harry is an Introvert. Now she wants to find out if he's a Perceiving or a Judging type.

> **TRACY:** There's a list of things I want to go over with you. Would you like to set up an exact time to meet, or would you prefer we keep it open?

HARRY: I'll take your memo home tonight and we can talk about it first thing tomorrow morning. Why don't we meet at 8:00 and get everything wrapped up by 10:00?

Because of the tight time schedules that Harry is setting up, Tracy knows that he is a Judging type. Tracy is aware that Harry may try to force premature closure on issues that are important to her:

TRACY: If we can get everything done in two hours great, but it may take longer. We'll give it our best shot.

Tracy still wants to find out two more things: Harry's Sensing/Intuitive and Thinking/Feeling index preferences.

TRACY: Would you prefer an overview, or details and specific problems and solutions?
HARRY: If you could include as many details as possible, that would be a big help.

Tracy has now found out that Harry is a Sensing type (which she had suspected from his 30/60/90-report requirements). Later, from talking with Alex and Paul, she learns that Harry is a Thinking type. Remarks like, "I planned on some whining and a few people taking off," are quintessential Thinking-type statements.

Before the Meeting

Tracy knows that each of her Personality Negotiating preferences are different from Harry's. Therefore, she must be careful to deal with Harry much differently than she would like to have people deal with her.

Specifically, before the meeting she'll make specific arguments that are practical and contain sufficient detail for Harry's Sensing preference. She'll show her written report to a Sensing/Thinking-type colleague in Boston before she sends it up to insure that it contains enough detail, practicality, and logical progression of thought.

At the Meeting

After expressing her concerns about the early morning meetings and the vast amount of time it takes her reps to complete the reports, she listens to Harry explain his reasons for implementing the rules.

After Harry explains his concerns, he also relays to her the fact that, since each of his branch managers has approached him on this matter, he considers it to be very important.

Step 1: List Concerns

The first thing Tracy does is list the concerns of all involved. She goes to his whiteboard and writes:

You	Branch Managers
1. That you get data you require from the branches to finish your reports to management.	1. That our sales force has the time they need to sell.
2. When sales reps are paid to work a 40-hour week, they do.	2. That management gets the data they request on time.
3. When reports come in they are not sloppy or inaccurate.	3. Keeping the attrition rate low so time and money don't have to be spent on training.
4. Increasing growth by the forecasted amount, while staying in budget.	4. Keeping the sales force motivated and feeling positive about the company.

Next, Tracy asks Harry if he has any other concerns. After about ten seconds, he tells her that he's concerned that the sales force isn't motivated, so she adds it to her list.

Step 2: Invent Options

Tracy begins inventing options with Harry. Since Harry is a Sensing type, she knows his instinct is to want to look only at a limited set of practical solutions, and will want to reject radical ones out of hand. She adapts to his style, but also must be true to her Intuitive nature.

> **TRACY:** Let's invent options so we reach the most effective solution. My goal is to have all your concerns addressed. I *know* there's a solution out there, and if we put our heads together, I know we can find it.
>
> We should focus on practical solutions, and at the very beginning we should not discount any option. Who knows? We may hit on something good. Is that okay with you?
>
> **HARRY:** Sure.

Tracy breaks Harry's concerns into four categories: 1) reports coming in late, 2) reports coming in messy, 3) the salespeople starting work late on Mondays, and 4) maintaining revenue increases. Tracy repeats to

Harry what she feels Harry's concerns are until he's satisfied that she understands what he wants.

Next, Tracy lumps her concerns into two categories: 1) time management of the sales force, and 2) morale.

The first thing Tracy wants to do is to gather some facts:

> **TRACY:** How long do you think it takes the salespeople to do the reports that you're requiring?
>
> **HARRY:** Judging from their sloppy quality, I'd say it takes them about fifteen minutes. Some of your colleagues say that it takes them all morning, but frankly, I don't believe them.
>
> **TRACY:** Writing the report takes them about a half hour, but getting the data takes them all morning. They know what their customers are going to buy, let's say, thirty days from now. But the forecasts of what's likely ninety days out take much longer.
>
> **HARRY:** Why should it? Don't they just ask their customers' purchasing departments? And if they already are going to all that effort, they're not doing a very good job. As a whole, their 90-day forecasts are horrendous. Our buyers have no idea what our inventory levels should be. We're either caught with too much product or a backorder situation.

Harry has been mulling over this problem for quite a while and has just done a mind dump. Since Harry's an Introvert, each concern is well thought out and needs to be addressed, which Tracy will now do:

> **TRACY:** You've brought out several important points. Let's not go any further until we talk about them. First, the reps can ask their customers' purchasing departments for orders that are thirty days out, because purchasing has already received the requisitions. That's why that data is always accurate.
>
> Beyond thirty days, things get murky. Because purchasing doesn't have the information, the reps have to go to the individual product managers and ask them what's in the approval pipeline. This means they may have to make over fifty calls—many times the managers aren't in and the reps have to call them back. This can take all morning and into lunch. Also, the product managers don't mind being called once a month, but when they get called every week, they pretty much give our reps the brush-off, and give seat-of-the-pants estimates rather than checking their records.

When we get to ninety days out, we're dealing with a very gray area because the product managers don't have approvals yet.

That's why the ninety-day forecasts are so inaccurate. That's also the reason why the reports take all morning, not just a few minutes. The reps want to give you accurate information, which often doesn't come in until lunchtime. We have to fax the reports to you by one o'clock, so often there's only a few minutes to pull it all together. Do you understand what I'm saying?

HARRY: Yes.

Tracy's arguments scored several times. She honed in on his Sensing, Thinking, and Judging preferences. First off, she didn't mention that the reps were griping the whole time, since that would have weakened her case. Then she wanted to convey: 1) the process that the reps follow is complex; 2) why the reports took all morning and not just a few minutes; 3) in that time, he can have complete data or attractive reports, but not both; 4) why the long-range forecasts were inaccurate; and 5) the groundwork for showing that the reps calling every week was bothering the customers.

> **TRACY:** Another concern you had is that the morale is low. Reps are apprehensive about calling their customers for the data when all the customers do is say things like, "Are you calling again?" or "Didn't you just ask me that a few days ago?" The sales reps are worried that annoyed customers will be ex-customers.
>
> They also know that you only need the data once a month, so they feel that they're spinning their wheels. They tell me they're wasting valuable time that would otherwise be spent getting new accounts or following through on current business.

Now Tracy is keying in on the "annoying the customers" concern she has. She also lays it out on the table that everyone knows that Harry only needs the data once a month. If getting the data were just a bother to his employees, he might say, "screw 'em." But he can't say that to customers, who can easily find another supplier.

Tracy is also laying the groundwork for her next point: that the time being spent on the reports is keeping the reps from selling. Harry's attitude had been that the reps were lazy complainers, and he is beginning to see that isn't true. Tracy's sprinting toward the finish line.

TRACY: Our reps are dedicated professionals, and are very thorough in their work. They're torn by having to choose between servicing their customers or servicing their company. When the reps feel the conflict is unsolvable, they leave to work for our competitor.

This means we have to spend money recruiting other sales reps, who I have to spend time interviewing and training—which I don't mind doing, it's part of my job. But it takes away time I think would be more productive helping reps get new accounts and meeting with customers.

Also, when our reps work for our competitor, they take their accounts with them. Our non-competition clause says they can't call their old customers first, but no one can stop the customers from calling them—which they are doing.

Tracy has won all her points. Harry's conflict resolution style is win–lose, yield–lose, compromise, collaborative, and lose–lose. He'll now go from win–lose to yield–lose:

HARRY: I guess you're right. Let's forget the whole thing. No more meetings, no more reports.

Tracy sees a yield–lose deal brewing. She doesn't accept it, and feels Harry is ready to invent solutions:

TRACY: That wouldn't be good, either, because you need input from us to do your job. Let's invent solutions so everyone can get their job done.

Harry sees this as an opportunity to compromise, which Tracy deflects:

HARRY: Why don't we have the reports come every other week?
TRACY: That's one suggestion to look at, but let's see if we can arrive at a solution that fulfills everyone's needs. You want the projections the third week of every month, right?
HARRY: Right.
TRACY: Our customers don't mind researching for us once a month, so why not have the salespeople get it on the second week of the month. That way if they're late, you'll still get it on time.
HARRY: That would work.
TRACY: Also, the time-consuming part of the reports is having to do a customer-by-customer breakdown. How about if I

meet with the reps and filter the data for you. That way we can give you an aggregate number on the forecasts. It will serve your needs to order inventory, and it won't take up the salespeople's time.

HARRY: That's okay, but I'm still concerned with the salespeople's getting to work at 10:00 Monday mornings.

TRACY: Why don't we give them an option: we can either have a 6:30 A.M. sales meeting, or we can have a mandatory working-lunch sales meeting that lasts an hour. This way, they'll be working an hour that they usually have off.

HARRY: If you don't mind giving up lunch, I don't mind.

TRACY: So, what we'll do is poll our customers once a month, and I'll give you a report that's an aggregate of the 30/60/90 buying plans of the customers in the branch. Also, we'll institute a mandatory Monday lunchtime sales meeting.

HARRY: Right. That's okay by me.

Tracy, using Personality Negotiating, accomplished what the others didn't. A key element in her negotiation was not letting Harry succumb to a losing deal at the end. Her putting forth a little more effort created a win–win deal out of a win–lose deal. The next case is a different type—it looks at how Judging and Perceiving types spend their vacation.

Case Study II—Perceiving and Judging Vacation-Day Schedules

This case involves looking at how a Judging and a Perceiving type spend a day of their vacations. A lot can be learned about each by the way they schedule their time. Let's say that our Judging and Perceiving types kept daily reminders or notes. How would your vacation day be similar to, or different from, these?

First, let's take a look at our Judging-type's calendar:

Wednesday, April 11

7:00	Wake up
7:30	Room-service breakfast ordered yesterday arrives on time
7:45	Go to hotel lobby for bus tour
8:00	Tour bus leaves

10:00	Finish tour
10:15	Relax in hotel for half hour
10:45	Relaxation time over—see Colosseum for last time—while at Colosseum decide on next city
11:30	Confirm hotel reservation (in Florence)
12:00	Eat lunch
1:00	See Vatican museums during 4-hour tour

And so on throughout the day.

The Perceiving type's day is next. Perceiving types won't make a schedule, but will play things by ear. Since this Perceiving type didn't have a watch on or look at a clock as he wrote his notes, he had no idea what time it was. Still, he had an interesting day. Here's how it went:

Got up.
Wandered around the streets and found a great little restaurant for breakfast.
Got lost on the city bus system, but saw lots of interesting sights including the Colosseum.
Ate lunch when I got hungry—happened to see the Pope pass by on the way.
Saw some of the Vatican museums—wanted to take long tour, but the doors closed at 5:00.
Saw the Colosseum again—it was much prettier in the moonlight.
Was going to Florence, but there was a regatta in Venice so changed my mind.

The Judging type's schedule is precise and includes decision deadlines. "Rome may not have been built in a day, but it could be seen in one," is the rallying cry of the Judging type. He wakes up at 7:00 and has breakfast at 7:30. He knew what he would have because he had placed his room-service order the night before. He didn't miss the tour bus because he was there early.

He had also decided that his morning visit to the Colosseum would be the last, and that a decision on the next day's plans needed to be made by 11:30. As a Judging type, he knew that the Vatican museum took four hours and that he would have to be there by 1:00. Meals were taken at pre-specified times, not when he was hungry.

The Perceiving type also had a great day in Rome. He may have spent time looking for breakfast, but found an excellent place. Getting lost on the city's bus system allowed him to see sights that those on tour busses would never see. He may have missed the Sistine Chapel, but did see other things (and the Pope). Finally, instead of going to Florence, he got to see the regatta in Venice that the Judging type missed.

The Judging type's vacation in Italy was predictable, while the Perceiving type's was spontaneous. Neither vacation is, in itself, better than the other. However, either way may be better for any particular person.

Case Study III—Type These Personalities

The final case study, below, is comprised of the personality profiles of two different people. Can you figure out their personality types from the clues given?

Personality Profile #1

> Brian Hood is an engineer for a defense contracting company. He designs antiaircraft guns, and is responsible for writing computer programs that run simulation tests before prototyping the weapons. These programs must be precise and he must have a mastery of many details about weapons systems.
>
> Brian's favorite part of the day is early morning, before everyone arrives at the office. During this time he gets the computer printouts the government sent him overnight and neatly arranges them in folders.
>
> One concern Brian has is that he would prefer to have a private office, which was lost due to budget cuts, and must now share an office with other people, which he finds noisy. Still, he reasons that although it's not the best situation, that's the way it needs to be.
>
> Brian is usually working on four or five projects at once, but knows each deadline and always finishes on time.

Have you figured out Brian's personality type?

Brian's Personality Type

Brian is an ISTJ, an Introverted, Sensing, Thinking, Judging type. Here are the clues that should have led you to that conclusion:

INTROVERT: Brian's favorite part of the day is the morning, before everyone arrives, and he prefers a private office because the noise in a crowded office is too distracting.

SENSING: The other reason morning is a good time for him is that it gives him a chance to organize the memos. His job requires mastery of details and precise calculations.

THINKING: When he lost his private office, he understood that that's the way it had to be. He doesn't take it as a personal insult. This is how Thinking types react.

JUDGING: He has a firm command of all his deadlines and never misses any. (This is a tough one to call with the limited information provided because Perceiving types who have jobs requiring many deadlines oftentimes manage to meet them. The difference is that meeting the deadline will be a struggle for Perceiving types and natural for Judging types.)

Personality Profile #2

> Helen Kramer is an editor of a newspaper in a small city in New Hampshire. She likes her job and does it well. Most of her editorials have to do with the plight of animals in shelters and the poor.
>
> She makes it a point to know each employee personally, and it seems as if she is always meeting with one group or another. Helen writes mostly about future solutions, and doesn't like to get too much into detail.
>
> She'll keep pushing on an issue relentlessly until something or someone changes things for the better.

Do you know Helen's personality type?

Helen's Personality Profile

Helen's personality type is an ENFP (Extroverted, Intuitive, Feeling, Perceiving type).

EXTROVERT: You know Helen is an Extrovert because she is always in meetings.

INTUITIVE: Intuitives, like Helen, like writing about general solutions and talking theoretically, leaving the details to others. If she were a Sensing type, she would frequently write very specific editorials with detailed solutions.

FEELING: We know she's a Feeling type because she wants to know all her employees. (If you thought it was because she wrote about the plight of animals and the homeless, that's not it. A Thinking type might write about collective groups, so until you had more information you couldn't guess.)

PERCEIVING: Helen's a Perceiving type because she has an event schedule—she keeps on writing relentlessly until something is done rather than pursuing this goal for a year and moving on to something else.

Now that you have confirmed or corrected your personality typing of Brian Hood and Helen Kramer, how would you negotiate with them? Look up complete and detailed information on negotiating with INTJ's, ENFP's, and the other types in the next chapter.

Conclusion

Find out as much as you can about people before the meeting so you can adapt your negotiation style to theirs. If people come out swinging with a win–lose style, remember that it's only one part of the conflict-resolution pattern. If you hold out, and Personality Negotiate, they'll be amenable to a win–win solution.

Chapter 8
NEGOTIATING WITH THE SIXTEEN PERSONALITY TYPES

You may have already figured out that with four areas of Personality Negotiating, each with a choice of two functions, there's a total of 2 × 2 × 2 × 2 or 16 different combinations of personality traits, or types.

Each person has one function in each of the four areas of Personality Negotiating that is preferred. Those of you who took the Negotiation Personality Guide at the back of this book or broken up into earlier chapters or the Myers-Briggs Type Indicator know your own four preferences. Even those who have not taken these tests can sometimes get a good idea of their preferences just by hearing the descriptions and typing themselves. Interestingly, many think, for example, that they are Extroverts because they like being with people, or they are Sensates because they are practical. Human beings are too complex to judge preferences on the basis of only one personality cue, because there are Introverts who like being with people and Intuitives who are practical. Remember, your and other's preferences are determined by how you *usually* react to situations. That's why you need to ask several questions and make a number of observations before and during a negotiation to know how to negotiate with someone.

Same-Type People Are Still Different

The MBTI categorizes sixteen different behavior combinations, but there are five billion people in the world, and each is a unique individual. People are simply too complex to clump them into even sixteen different groups and expect them to act the same way. Personality Negotiating uses the Jungian type-theory measurements because the MBTI is, at present, the best predictor of how people want to be dealt with, but it isn't meant to label individuals or their behaviors in every situation.

Preference 1	Preference 2	Preference 3	Preference 4	Type	Percentage of American Population
E/I	S/N	T/F	J/P		

				ESTJ	14.17
		T	J		
			P	ESTP	14.17
	S				
		F	J	ESFJ	14.17
			P	ESFP	14.17
E					
		T	J	ENTJ	4.77
			P	ENTP	4.77
	N				
		F	J	ENFJ	4.77
			P	ENFP	4.77

		T	J	ISTJ	4.77
			P	ISTP	4.77
	S				
		F	J	ISFJ	4.77
			P	ISFP	4.77
I					
		T	J	INTJ	1.67
			P	INTP	1.67
	N				
		F	J	INFJ	1.67
			P	INFP	1.67

Makeup of personality types

What Is Your "Dominant" Function?

Psychologists say that everyone has a dominant function and an inferior function. An important part of Personality Negotiating is recognizing and adapting your negotiating style to focus on others' "dominant" or favorite function while avoiding their "inferior" or least favorite function. The dominant function is a preference from index two or three, either Sensing or Intuitive, Thinking or Feeling, that is the best developed—that is, the one the person relies on most. The key to identifying a person's dominant, as well as secondary, tertiary and inferior functions, is his or her preferences on the Introvert/Extrovert and Judging/Perceiving indexes. Extroverted Judging types have their third index preference as their dominant function, while Extroverted Perceiving types have their second index preference dominant.

Introverts are opposite. Introverted Judging types have their second index preference dominant, while Extroverted Perceiving types have the third index preference dominant.

Preferences				Dominant (inferior) Function	
Index 1 E/I		Index 4 J/P		Index 2 S/N	Index 3 T/F
Extrovert	+	Judging	=	____	Thinking or Feeling
Extrovert	+	Perceiving	=	Sensing or Intuitive	____
Introvert	+	Judging	=	Sensing or Intuitive	____
Introvert	+	Perceiving	=	____	Thinking or Feeling

The secondary function is the person's "other" middle index preference. The inferior function is the function that is opposite the dominant and is the weakest and least developed.

When negotiating, concentrate your efforts on the dominant and secondary functions and away from the inferior function. For instance an ENTJ (Extroverted, Intuitive, Thinking, Judging type) has a dominant Thinking function and inferior Feeling function. Sell an ENTJ on the impersonal logic of the solution (the dominant Thinking function) and not the happiness and harmony the solution will generate (the inferior Feeling function).

The Importance of the Dominant Function

The dominant function is the function that must be focused on to get to the heart of people's concerns. If someone has a Sensing dominant function he won't commit until he has all the facts and is sure that what he is agreeing to is practical.

How Perceiving Types Decide

Negotiating to the dominant function is especially important when you're dealing with Perceiving types, because they are careful decision makers. If the issue of the negotiations directly relates to the dominant function of a Perceiving type, it's essential to address that function during the negotiation. If Perceiving types are considering something outside their dominant function, they'll value it as less important and usually make the decision easily. For instance, suppose a Perceiving type with a Feeling dominant function (INFP or ISFP) is negotiating the purchase of office supplies. The decision will be made quickly, for example, which wastebaskets or staplers to buy because such things won't do much, if anything, to affect office harmony or job satisfaction. The decision will be an easy one. However, if that same Perceiving-Feeling-type individual is responsible for negotiating with insurance companies and comparing the scope of employee benefits, he or she will have a very stressful time deciding—even if the competing companies' plans are very similar. The dominant Feeling function would kick in, and that individual would become personally involved, worrying that every nuance of the benefit packages under consideration is a potential disaster.

When you discover your dominant function and the dominant functions of those with whom you are dealing, your job and theirs will be much easier.

The Sixteen Different Personality Types

Putting It All Together

Putting all the personality trait combinations together, however, provides more information than concentrating on any single preference. One gains much more insight into the person on the other side of the table by taking into consideration the combination of preferences as a whole.

Here are descriptions of how to negotiate with each of the sixteen different personality types. Each description is complete and covers several different areas of interest to negotiators. They are:

1. **The types' dominant, secondary, tertiary, and inferior functions.** This will help you know what to expect from individuals of the type and how to negotiate with them.

   An important point to remember: The function that you *observe*, that is, the way someone acts, is called *Extroverted* behavior for both Extroverts and Introverts. You'll notice the dominant function for Extroverts, but the secondary function for Introverts. The following will help explain this concept.

   > ESTP's (Extroverted, Sensing, Thinking, Perceiving types) have a dominant Sensing function and a secondary Thinking function. You can expect them to ask questions about facts but think to themselves, "How logical is this?"

   > ESTJ's (Extroverted, Sensing, Thinking, Judging types) have a dominant Thinking function and a secondary Sensing function. You can expect ESTJ's to ask how logical a solution is but think to themselves, "What details are missing?"

   > ISTP's (Introverted, Sensing, Thinking, Perceiving types) have a dominant Thinking function that's introverted. Their function pattern looks similar to the ESTP, asking questions about the facts of a system while thinking to themselves, "What's the logical relationship among the facts?"

   > ISTJ's (Introverted, Sensing, Thinking, Judging types) have a dominant and introverted Sensing function and a secondary Thinking function. This means that their function pattern will be similar to the ESTJ, asking questions about the logic behind the facts and thinking to themselves, "What are the missing details?"

2. **The occupations in which the type predominates.** This will give you an idea of the kind of work and work environment each type prefers and the type of people that gravitate towards specific professions.
3. **Strengths.**
4. **Weaknesses.**
5. **Negotiation Busters.** What to *avoid doing* at all costs, because they will irritate or annoy these individuals so much they may refuse to negotiate with you.
6. **How to negotiate with the type.** This section provides a template of how to conduct a successful negotiation. You'll notice that the strategies are far different, depending on the type.

NOTE: Based on your type, examine your own preferred negotiation style. There may be things about the way others negotiate that disturb you, but you can't quite put your finger on them. Just as the people you deal with are particular about their favorite ways to negotiate, so are you. If others are negotiating outside your preferred style, talk to them. Let them know how to negotiate with you—what they can do to make the negotiations easier and move along more smoothly.

ESTJ

Dominant	**Thinking**
Secondary	Sensing
Tertiary	Intuitive
Inferior	Feeling

ESTJ OCCUPATIONS: banker, manager, accountant, insurance executive.

STRENGTHS: ESTJ's make sound, practical, and responsible decisions. They'll want your solutions to make logical sense, but they will be concerned with details.

Present them with neatly organized, practical ideas. New, unconventional strategies won't succeed. ENTJ's are less concerned about how people feel about a decision, and more concerned with practicality. They won't commit to "foolish," impractical, or overbudget deals.

WEAKNESSES: ESTJ's are inclined to reject new proposals and untried solutions or products. They might reject proposals on appearance, instead of on merit. They often don't give positive feedback when a person goes "above and beyond," assuming that the continued relationship alone is acknowledgement enough of a job well done.

NEGOTIATION BUSTERS: ESTJ's don't like it when people can't speak intelligently and confidently during the negotiation. Proposals need to be pristine. Present traditional, conservative solutions. New ideas need support from factual evidence.

HOW TO NEGOTIATE WITH THE ESTJ: Prepare well organized, neatly presented proposals rich in detail and documentation, and go over them together line by line. If you don't know an answer, rather than guess tell them you'll get back to them. Don't "wing it" because ESTJ's are very good at logical analysis of facts, and one wrong guess can lose their confidence.

ESTP

Dominant	Sensing
Secondary	Thinking
Tertiary	Feeling
Inferior	Intuitive

ESTP OCCUPATIONS: marketing, police work, construction worker, farmer, auditor.

STRENGTHS: ESTP's analyze facts and can understand a large amount of information very quickly. Although they are distracted by "Intuitive" or "unorganized" presentations, they'll look for value in them. Working with or discussing tangible problems or situations which have significant immediate impact is what this type likes. They find talking about highly theoretical concepts or far-off future plans tedious.

WEAKNESSES: Ideas or presentations that rely heavily on theory, have no immediate application, and don't include models will be a tough sell. If ESTP's can't use their dominant Sensing function, they won't accept that a solution is viable.

NEGOTIATION BUSTERS: Getting too theoretical. Not proving the workability of concepts by basing them on working model or trying them out somehow—even if only on a small scale. Negotiating issues too far into the future for the ESTP to care.

HOW TO NEGOTIATE WITH THE ESTP: Prepare a thorough, well-organized presentation showing practical benefit. If possible, provide prototype or model proving feasibility of solution.

ESFJ

Dominant	Feeling
Secondary	Sensing
Tertiary	Intuitive
Inferior	Thinking

ESFJ OCCUPATIONS: secretary, teacher, salesperson, nurse, hairdresser, office manager.

STRENGTHS: ESFJ's get along well with others and are great on teamwork. They are often the catalysts in bringing negotiators with diverse opinions together. They're friendly, organized, and realistic. They like harmony and practicality and lead by example. People cooperate with ESFJ's because they want to, not because they have to.

WEAKNESSES: They want tranquillity and loathe conflict. When negotiations become stalemated or beleaguered by animosity, they may throw in the towel. They combine factual analysis with human interactions instead of logical analysis, so their preferred decision process often differs from what is expected in business.

NEGOTIATION BUSTERS: Placing too much emphasis on logic, or "new ideas." Proposing solutions that will cause inconvenience, or presenting solutions that will bring short-term or long-term stress during transition.

HOW TO NEGOTIATE WITH THE ESFJ: Show them benefits people will enjoy and the practicality of coming to an agreement. Those who dress impeccably and fashionably will be viewed more positively than those who take fashion risks.

ESFP

Dominant	Sensing
Secondary	Feeling
Tertiary	Thinking
Inferior	Intuitive

ESFP OCCUPATIONS: Child care worker, receptionist, transportation worker, engineer, site supervisor, lifeguard.

STRENGTHS: ESFP's love being with other people and are adept noticers of details about people and things. They're warm, witty, and outstanding conversationalists. Their combination of realism and concern for others makes them excellent crisis solvers, so they are often seen as the mediators in negotiations. They'll notice but will overlook missing details.

WEAKNESSES: ESFP's like to work in groups. They find working alone to be very difficult. They prefer projects that are practical and have immediate human benefit, and won't put much credence in analytical and impersonal data.

NEGOTIATION BUSTERS: Sloppy or unattractive presentations will bother the ESFP. Focusing on logic or theory alone will seem cold and won't work well with them. Also, ESFP's will not allow one-sided deals or one side steamrolling the other to happen.

HOW TO NEGOTIATE WITH THE ESFP: Prepare a high appearance proposal and dress classically and impeccably. In-person negotiations are a must. Present solutions that will benefit both parties and explain why each side will benefit.

ENFP

Dominant   Intuitive
Secondary   Feeling
Tertiary   Thinking
Inferior   Sensing

ENFP OCCUPATIONS: journalist, cleric, social worker, teacher.

STRENGTHS: ENFP types are usually involved in a wide range of activities—simultaneously. They love discussing alternatives and theories, and will look at as many options as you care to discuss with them but their Sensing inferior function can cause them to become easily bored by details and practicality.

When making important decisions, ENFP's will insist on and enjoy looking at all the possibilities before deciding. They are easy to deal with and look for the good things in people; this makes them very good at team-building.

WEAKNESSES: Because they're involved in so much at any one time, they might overlook details about any given solution. They may discover after the fact that they made a decision without carefully examining practicality and find themselves with an unworkable situation. They tend to delay decision making and change their interests frequently.

NEGOTIATION BUSTERS: Don't overwhelm an ENFP with details. Because of their sociability, you'll have much more success meeting with them than sending them information to look at privately. ENFP's will not like it if you ignore how people involved feel about a situation or if you refuse to look at alternatives.

HOW TO NEGOTIATE WITH THE ENFP: ENFP's will want to talk about your solution in outline, not in detail. They'll be concerned that the people affected by their decision will like it. If negotiations begin to drag on too long, you'll have to remind ENFP's that alternatives can be examined forever. Show them the benefits of committing sooner rather than later.

ENFJ

Dominant	Feeling
Secondary	Intuitive
Tertiary	Sensing
Inferior	Thinking

ENFJ OCCUPATIONS: cleric, teacher, actor, writer, counselor.

STRENGTHS: ENFJ's make great leaders and see the possibilities in people. They encourage harmony and cooperation and are appreciative and adaptable. They're excellent communicators and lead by example.

WEAKNESSES: ENFJ's may see too much in people and expect things beyond a person's reach. They tend to avoid negotiations that involve conflict. ENFJ's need to make sure that plans are logical and practical before undertaking them.

NEGOTIATION BUSTERS: Avoid putting too much emphasis on the logic behind a solution, why it can be expected to work, or its long-term benefits. ENFJ's will want to see immediate, tangible results and happiness and harmony as by-products of the negotiation.

HOW TO NEGOTIATE WITH THE ENFJ: Focus on how solutions benefit people. Prepare and discuss overviews and have a plan for implementation.

ENTP

Dominant	Intuitive
Secondary	Thinking
Tertiary	Feeling
Inferior	Sensing

ENTP OCCUPATIONS: photographer, marketing, salesperson, journalist, actor, engineer.

STRENGTHS: ENTP's are excellent problem solvers and like having complex problems to work on. They excel at developing solutions to conceptual problems. They lead by example and encouragement.

WEAKNESSES: Although ENTP's are good at problem solving, they are not so adept with mundane, non-theoretical negotiations. They some-times underestimate the time it takes to complete a negotiation or project, and can set false expectations.

NEGOTIATION BUSTERS: Focusing on details or feelings or refusing to discuss possibilities for solutions.

HOW TO NEGOTIATE WITH THE ENTP: Discuss with them theoretical possibilities of the agreement. Focus on the big picture and on logic and objectivity.

ENTJ

Dominant **Thinking**
Secondary Intuitive
Tertiary   Sensing
Inferior   Feeling

ENTJ OCCUPATIONS: manager, lawyer, marketing, salesperson, other professionals involved in problem solving.

STRENGTHS: ENTJ's are very good at solving problems, building struc-tures in organizations, and leading. In group negotiations ENTJ's are seen taking command of the group. They like to have ideas presented in logical form, and are eager to consider many different suggested solu-tions. After you sell an ENTJ on an idea, he or she will be very good about following through with a commitment.

ENTJ's tend to make decisions impersonally, especially if they don't know the people involved, so they may need to be made aware of the human impact of their decisions.

WEAKNESSES: ENTJ's are not good at grasping details and dislike procedure. Their inferior Feeling function can sometimes make deci-sions seem uncaring. Since this could hurt them in the long run, ENTJ's should make an effort to consider the human element in any decision.

Also, if there are two ENTJ's involved in a negotiation, they could have a dominance contest. ENTJ's want to come to closure so quickly, they could leave people out of the information loop.

NEGOTIATION BUSTERS: Sending information to ENTJ's with no dis-cussion will get limited attention. Details and facts unrelated to logical conclusions will be ignored and will distract the ENTJ from your pre-sentation.

HOW TO NEGOTIATE WITH THE ENTJ: Suggest several different solutions, and consult with the ENTJ on the best one. The presentation should be sound logically and be forward-looking. Present facts and details only if they are necessary for a logical decision. ENTJ's like to talk about solutions and will respond well to people who seem unequivocal in their resolve.

ISTJ

Dominant	Sensing
Secondary	Thinking
Tertiary	Feeling
Inferior	Intuitive

ISTJ OCCUPATIONS: president, chairman of the board, banker, insurance executive, accountant, bookkeeper, adjuster, engineer.

STRENGTHS: According to *Fortune* magazine, 35 percent of all upper-level managers are ISTJ's.[1] Individuals of this type have a profound sense of detail and logical analysis.

Their Introverted Sensing preferences make them good at analysis. Like the ESTJ, the ISTJ wants conservative, well-thought-out ideas presented clearly and neatly.

ISTJ's are sometimes averse to new ideas because of their traditional mind-set and their inferior Intuitive function. They are inclined to view anything untraditional very skeptically. ISTJ's can dissect large amounts of data expertly. When they are given adequate time to reflect, their decisions are generally responsible and cost-effective, and prove to be good ones. ISTJ's seldom make factual mistakes.

WEAKNESSES: ISTJ's like poring over data privately and sometimes appear aloof. If they are in positions that require meetings, make sure you meet with them early in the day—or later after everyone else has gone home.

NEGOTIATION BUSTERS: Calling them at "inappropriate" times (when they want to concentrate, which is usually the case). ISTJ's dislike poorly organized and presented proposals, and "wild ideas," especially those without factual support.

HOW TO NEGOTIATE WITH THE ISTJ: Prepare highly detailed, well-supported, organized, and neat proposals and send them to the ISTJ before the meeting. This gives them time to go over the proposals privately and in depth, so they will fully understand and appreciate your suggestions. Schedule meetings well in advance. ISTJ's view unsolicited phone calls and unscheduled meetings as unwelcome interruptions.

At meetings, give them time to speak. Make sure that meetings don't run unnecessarily long.

ISTP

Dominant **Thinking**
Secondary Sensing
Tertiary Intuitive
Inferior Feeling

ISTP OCCUPATIONS: military personnel, farmer, mechanic, engineer, dental hygienist, programmer.

STRENGTHS: ISTP's are superior troubleshooters. They make excellent spontaneous decisions and respond quickly and correctly in the midst of crisis—some of the greatest generals were ISTP's. They have an outstanding ability to analyze information and to act instinctively and properly.

WEAKNESSES: Becoming bored in non-crisis negotiations, ISTP's will want to wrap them up quickly and move on to something more exciting. They may neglect people's feelings or new possibilities.

NEGOTIATION BUSTERS: ISTP's are put off by long, drawn out, tedious negotiations. Having large meetings or talking about theory won't work well with them, either.

HOW TO NEGOTIATE WITH THE ISTP: If your suggestion helps solve a crisis, it's likely to be a short negotiation. Send the ISTP a copy of your ideas detailing immediate benefit. Present your information neatly and logically.

ISFJ

Dominant **Sensing**
Secondary Feeling
Tertiary Thinking
Inferior Intuitive

ISFJ OCCUPATIONS: nurse, teacher, librarian, physician, middle manager, secretary.

STRENGTHS: ISFJ's like jobs that are traditional. They prefer to work in positions where they can be useful to others. They have great organizational skills, but dislike jobs that require only systems and factual analysis. ISFJ's, unlike ISTJ's, usually won't gravitate toward upper management because they prefer working for someone else. The ISFJ's greatest strength is analyzing facts in a personal way. They have the keen ability to distill information because of their ISJ, but having Feeling as their secondary function helps them put the data into human terms.

WEAKNESSES: ISFJ's inferior function is Intuition. Although their goal is developing solutions that people like, they have difficulty considering ideas that are non-traditional.

NEGOTIATION BUSTERS: ISFJ's won't respond well to "cold-hearted" presentations or "way-out" ideas during a negotiation. They could also be easily overwhelmed by Extroverted presentations, especially if the presentation is theoretical, not factual, in nature.

HOW TO NEGOTIATE WITH THE ISFJ: Before a meeting give the ISFJ a detailed proposal to read that 1) shows the practical benefit of your solution and, 2) covers the concerns of the various affected parties so the ISFJ is assured that everyone will be satisfied with the suggested agreement.

ISFP

Dominant	Feeling
Secondary	Sensing
Tertiary	Intuitive
Inferior	Thinking

ISFP OCCUPATIONS: stock clerk, surveyor, mechanic, dental assistant, nurse, secretary.

STRENGTHS: ISFP's like harmonious environments and strive to have people enjoy their work. They'll come to agreements that are people-oriented and practical.

WEAKNESSES: Although ISFP's may notice things they don't like, they won't mention them for harmony's sake. They can't be swayed easily by analytical arguments.

NEGOTIATION BUSTERS: ISFP's don't like solutions that will cause people to be anxious. Negotiators shouldn't overwhelm ISFP's with theoretical, or new, ideas or have large, disruptive meetings with them.

HOW TO NEGOTIATE WITH THE ISFP: Prepare an attractive package in advance and show a written copy of the presentation to the ISFP. Include within the presentation practical ways to increase harmony immediately.

INFJ

Dominant	**Intuitive**
Secondary	Feeling
Tertiary	Thinking
Inferior	Sensing

INFJ OCCUPATIONS: clergy, teacher, social worker, librarian, scientist.

STRENGTHS: INFJ's are very good at developing and promoting harmony within a group. Their dominant Intuitive function allows them to explore possibilities as fast as you can present them to them. INFJ's are excellent at taking ideas, synthesizing them, and making the plans happen. They are invaluable in a negotiation, if you're fortunate enough to have them present. They form collaborative solutions easily and naturally.

WEAKNESSES: INFJ's dislike being overwhelmed with details and impersonal analysis. This is especially true when presented without a plan for implementation or when they aren't given time to reflect privately. One-sided deals will be apparent to them, and they will use their persuasive power to insure a fair agreement.

NEGOTIATION BUSTERS: Turn-offs with the INFJ include focusing on details and excluding the human element in a negotiation. Not having specific plans or being too analytical will not be effective with an INFJ.

HOW TO NEGOTIATE WITH THE INFJ: Show the INFJ your proposal beforehand, and focus on the idea that people will be benefitted quickly.

INFP

Dominant	**Feeling**
Secondary	Intuitive
Tertiary	Sensing
Inferior	Thinking

INFP OCCUPATIONS: psychiatrist, editor, journalist, teacher, social worker.

STRENGTHS: INFP's are excellent at team building and creating group harmony. They are inclined to be idealistic and not very materialistic. They are the most careful decision makers of any type, and they will carefully debate alternatives internally until a decision can be made that will promote harmony. They like solutions that will please people and developing strategies for easy and workable change. INFP's have excellent ideas, but their Introverted nature often requires that you ask their opinions on matters.

WEAKNESSES: INFP's focus on being careful might cause them to ignore the negative consequences of not coming to a decision, especially when there are people emotionally involved in the situation. They won't feel comfortable with closure related to the Feeling function unless they are sure that those they're deciding for (including themselves) will be happy with the outcome.

NEGOTIATION BUSTERS: Criticism, rushing a decision, too much Extroverted enthusiasm, and ignoring the feelings of people involved in a decision.

HOW TO NEGOTIATE WITH THE INFP: Find out quickly if the decision relates to their dominant function, Feeling. If it does, make sure that all involved are happy with the negotiations and discover, with them, possibilities for making everyone comfortable with the decision. If the issue doesn't relate to their dominant Feeling function, they are likely make their decisions quickly.

Don't bog the INFP down with details. Send them information to review before any meeting. Make meetings short, and make sure they're scheduled well in advance.

INFP's are always searching for meaning in the things others say and do. They might interpret an impersonal comment as personal criticism. If your solution has negative consequences, don't brush them off, deal with them.

INTJ

Dominant	Intuitive
Secondary	Thinking
Tertiary	Feeling
Inferior	Sensing

INTJ OCCUPATIONS: attorney, scientist, researcher, programmer, photographer, manager.

STRENGTHS: They'll grasp new ideas quickly and easily. INTJ's will be very good at developing plans for small groups. INTJ's, like ENTJ's, are excellent at understanding ideas. They are more likely to lead followers to their goals by example and are usually more autonomous than ENTJ's.

WEAKNESSES: They don't want presentations that are rich in detail, even when discussing plans or issue that merit detail. Sometimes INTJ's are so good at analytical reasoning that they can "reason out" the people involved in a decision.

NEGOTIATION BUSTERS: Focusing in on details, too much emphasis placed on non-analytical, emotional arguments, and not allowing for the Introverted thought process to take place.

HOW TO NEGOTIATE WITH THE INTJ: Prepare presentations in advance. Send the INTJ your conceptual ideas so that they can mull them over. Give them time to respond to questions during meetings. Make sure solutions for the INTJ let them lead, but without too much public interaction.

INTP

Dominant	Thinking
Secondary	Intuitive
Tertiary	Sensing
Inferior	Feeling

INTP OCCUPATIONS: chemist, writer, artist, researcher, programmer, lawyer, scientist.

STRENGTHS: INTP's are good at creating—whether systems, plans, or buildings. They're excellent problem solvers, but prefer to look for solutions early. Instead of being crisis managers, they foresee problems and develop logical and workable solutions far in advance of other types.

If INTP's are negotiating because they feel that there are long-term problems to be addressed, listen carefully. They are often right.

WEAKNESSES: INTP's like theoretical problems as opposed to immediate problems and prefer dealing with problems calmly over a long period, rather than fire-fighting.

NEGOTIATION BUSTERS: INTP's don't like presentations focused on practicality, emotion, or with strict time frames. They much prefer being in low-stress environments where productivity isn't measured in the amount of work completed.

HOW TO NEGOTIATE WITH THE INTP: Send them proposals that focus on logical and objective reasoning covering theoretical possibilities. Plan for a long negotiation that eventually will come through.

Conclusion

The first and fourth index preferences determine a person's dominant, secondary, tertiary and inferior functions (second and third index functions). For IJ and EP types, the dominant function is in the second index and the other functions follow clockwise. For EJ and IP types, the

Preferences			Dominant (inferior) Function	
Index 1 **E/I**	Index 4 **J/P**		Index 2 **S/N**	Index 3 **T/F**
Introvert	+ Judging	=	Sensing or Intuitive	____
Extrovert	+ Perceiving	=	Sensing or Intuitive	____

ISTJ

```
        S——T
   I  /      \  J
      |  →   |
      |  → ↓ |
       n    F
```

ENFP

```
        N——F
   E  /      \  P
      |  →   |
      |  → ↓ |
       s    T
```

Sensing types

	With Thinking	**With Feeling**
Introverts — **Judging types**	**ISTJ** I Mull decisions privately S Look for practicality T Do logical analysis J Decide on time deadline	**ISFJ** I Mull decisions privately S Look for practicality F Do human analysis J Decide on time deadline
Introverts — **Perceiving types**	**ISTP** I Mull decisions privately S Look for practicality T Do logical analysis P Decide on event deadline	**ISFP** I Mull decisions privately S Look for practicality F Do human analysis P Decide on event deadline
Extroverts — **Perceiving types**	**ESTP** E Verbalize thoughts S Look for practicality T Do logical analysis P Decide on event deadline	**ESFP** E Verbalize thoughts S Look for practicality F Do human analysis P Decide on event deadline
Extroverts — **Judging types**	**ESTJ** E Verbalize thoughts S Look for practicality T Do logical analysis J Decide on time deadline	**ESFJ** E Verbalize thoughts S Look for practicality F Do human analysis J Decide on time deadline

Table of behavioral traits

Intuitive types

With Feeling

With Thinking

Introverts

Judging types

INFJ
I Mull decisions privately
N Look for possibilities
F Do a human analysis
J Decide on time deadline

INTJ
I Mull decisions privately
N Look for possibilities
T Do logical analysis
J Decide on time deadline

Perceiving types

INFP
I Mull decisions privately
N Look for possibilities
F Do a human analysis
P Decide on event deadline

INTP
I Mull decisions privately
N Look for possibilities
T Do logical analysis
P Decide on event deadline

Extroverts

Perceiving types

ENFP
E Verbalize thoughts
N Look for possibilities
F Do human analysis
P Decide on event deadline

ENTP
E Verbalize thoughts
N Look for possibilities
T Do logical analysis
P Decide on event deadline

Judging types

ENFJ
E Verbalize thoughts
N Look for possibilities
F Do human analysis
J Decide on time deadline

ENTJ
E Verbalize thoughts
N Look for possibilities
T Do logical analysis
J Decide on time deadline

dominant function is in the third index and the other functions follow counterclockwise as shown.

Preferences					Dominant (inferior) Function	
Index 1 **E/I**		Index 4 **J/P**			Index 2 **S/N**	Index 3 **T/F**
Extrovert	+	Judging	=		____	Thinking or Feeling
Introvert	+	Perceiving	=		____	Thinking or Feeling

ESTJ

```
      S ——— T
    /  ┌────←───┐  \
 E /   │        │   \ J
       ↓        │
       └───→────┘
   N        f
```

INFP

```
      N ——— F
    /  ┌────←───┐  \
 I /   │        │   \ P
       ↓        │
       └───→────┘
   S        t
```

When negotiating, focus your attention on your and others' dominant function, and avoid inferior function areas. Perceiving types will set up an event schedule, and won't commit until their dominant function has been appeased.

When you know what someone's personality type is, use Personality Negotiating to focus on the strengths, while avoiding negotiation busters.

NOTE

1. Moore, "Personality Tests Are Back."

Chapter 9
SUCCESSFUL STRATEGIES FOR DIFFERENT RELATIONSHIPS

Successful negotiation strategies depend on understanding the personality types of the people we are dealing with. But there are other important dimensions in negotiations—one of which is managing relationships. This chapter focuses on how to effectively manage ongoing and short-term interactions.

Instinctively, it shouldn't shock you that negotiations with your boss are different from ones with your subordinates. One reason for this is that in each situation your power and authority base is different.

In any chain of command, the power and authority structure is usually well defined. In the military, you know who the boss is—the one with the most stars on his or her shoulder. In a karate class, it's the one with the black belt. In business, you can tell the bosses by title, office size or location, who gets driven to work in a limo and who has to take the subway, and so on.

Animals have power structures, too. We get the term top dog from the canines who fight to see who gets to be the leader of the pack. Pecking order's etymology comes from chickens battling to get to eat first.

Although people with authority often have power, there's a difference between authority and power. Authority is the accepted structure in which members show deference to those above them. Power is an ability to coerce others into doing things you want them to do. A benign form of power is referent power—when you willingly do things for people because they've done you favors or treated you well. A hostile form of power is firing people a week before they become vested to avoid paying promised benefits.

A power play is a transaction that occurs when you act in a way to coerce someone else to act some way or do or say something very specific. This type of behavior is frequently seen as a by-product of poor negotiators who aren't getting their way, or don't see the value or necessity of collaborative solutions. We'll look at that now.

Power Plays

Hockey players experience power plays after someone is given a penalty. Depending on the seriousness of the infraction, the player has to sit isolated and out of action for a few minutes. During that time, the other team's extra player advantage allows them to execute what is known as a power play. They usually score during the power play because of their advantage over the other team. Psychologists co-opted the term from the sports world to mean what happens when one person has the upper hand over someone else. There are three types of power that can be played: One-up, one-down, and even.[1]

One-Up Power Plays

One-up power occurs when one party can bully the other party. An example of one-up power is the drill sergeant who makes recruits do push-ups and midnight runs for not obeying orders.

In business, few people have unlimited power to do as they like. Businesses only have one-up power if they're monopolies. The electric company used to be a non-regulated monopoly. If they wanted to, they could coerce people by threatening to shut off their power. Today, government regulation protects customers against monopolistic companies exerting one-up power over customers.

Everyone in business and government has to answer to someone. The chairman of the board of the biggest corporation has to answer to the stockholders. Even the president of the United States needs to answer to Congress.

Still, people, in theory, have one-up power over others. For example, a boss could fire a subordinate in a recession. Although the subordinate is free to work elsewhere, he or she will have difficulty finding a job. Like the hockey team that has more players on the ice, people who abuse one-up power attempt to get what they want using force.

> **FRANK:** I want you here at 5:00 a.m. and I don't want you to leave until after 6:00 p.m. Also, I want you to drive me to and pick me up from the airport. If you don't like it, quit. It will take you six months to find a job, and I'll have you replaced in an hour.

Usually, companies are dependent on their employees, so power is not absolute and a more moderate approach is taken.

> **KERRY:** I know we need more people, but we don't have the budget. Could you work some overtime until we get the quarterly reports finished?

One-Down Power Plays

One-down power plays occur when one party doesn't have the authority to exercise force over another. The one-down uses guerrilla techniques and indirect methods to get what he or she wants. First graders, for example, don't have coercive power over their teachers, but can get even with them by saying things they know will get their parents to angrily call the school superintendent. Here, the recipient of Frank's one-up power play (above) uses a one-down power play to "get even" with his boss:

> Greg, Frank's employee, is upset over being coerced into driving his boss to the airport. As he returns to the office, Frank's wife calls. Although Greg knows that Frank is alone on a business trip, he tells Frank's wife:
>
> "I'm sorry, he's not here right now. He'll be on vacation for a few days. I saw him leave with his wife about an hour ago."
>
> Greg used his one-down power to hurt Frank by making his wife suspicious.

One-down power is a very strong weapon used by people who are harmed and want to even the score. They will use one-down power to sabotage the person or parties that are dominating them. One-down power is very effective and must be respected. The person executing a one-down power play does nothing to alleviate his or her own situation, and would attain much more by negotiation. Still, many feel the psychological satisfaction of sabotage is worth it.

Even-Power Plays

Even-power plays occur when neither party has power to coerce the other blatantly. Like a chess match when both players start with the same amount of power, one must outmaneuver one's opponent. When there's an even-power play you'll see adversaries looking for weaknesses in their opponents and striking hard when they can.

In addition to power, another dimension in negotiations is authority. We'll look at that next.

Authority

Authority is different from power. Authority is one's genuine need to exert responsibility. When one exercises authority one is doing so in the best interests of all involved. In the military, knowing who's in charge is very important. When in battle, soldiers find it comforting to know who's in charge and what's expected of them.

Knowing *who* has the authority to do *what* is important during any negotiation. Without that knowledge, attention is taken off the issues and put on procedural matters distracting the interested parties from working together.

This chapter talks about how to use your and other's authority to get things done. The next chapter, Negotiating with Difficult People, talks about negotiating with people who misuse power and insist on throwing their weight around.

Win–Win Negotiating

The basis of Personality Negotiating is a "win–win" strategy. Simply put, win–win means that everyone leaves the negotiation better off than when they entered it. There are four possible outcomes to every negotiation. They are:

	PERSON A	PERSON B
WIN–WIN	WINS	WINS
WIN–LOSE	WINS	LOSES
LOSE–WIN	LOSES	WINS
LOSE–LOSE	LOSES	LOSES

In reality, it is only with the win–win outcome that anyone comes out ahead. As we saw earlier through the Frank and Greg scenario, if one party loses (win–lose or lose–win outcome) there is a tendency for the losing party to want to get even. The bottom line is that anything but win–win negotiations degrades to lose–lose eventually.

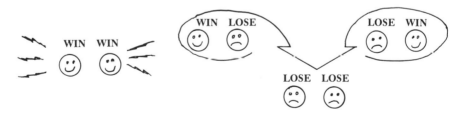

Following is another example of what happens when there's a win–lose negotiation.

Why Win–Lose Negotiating Doesn't Work

Riley Smithson is the president of Smithson Wheelchairs, Inc., a company that sells wheelchairs and other assistive devices to the disabled. After many successful years of having a primarily disabled sales force, Riley notices that his travel expenses are much higher than his competitors'. This is because the disabled reps need to buy more costly plane tickets and have special hotel rooms.

Riley decides not to lay any of his current salespeople off, but decides to hire only non-disabled salespeople in the future.

The existing sales force becomes irate when they hear of the new policy and try to negotiate a change. Riley explains how the company exceeds the affirmative-action requirements by several hundred percent and that he needs to get experienced salespeople who are not disabled to save on travel and expenses (T&E).

Soon after the announcement, the sales force starts complaining to their customers. They aren't selling much now because, instead of making sales calls, they're commiserating with each other. Eventually, their commissions fall, and many unhappy reps find other work.

After getting wind of the new policy, Smithson's competitor, Wheelright, sees the situation as an opportunity for a marketing boom.

Wheelright hires all the disabled salespeople he can away from Smithson, who replaces them with non-disabled salespeople. Wheelright then positions Smithson as a company who doesn't care about the disabled, and only wants their money.

The negative campaign works, and Smithson goes out of business after having been in business for many years.

Why Win–Win Negotiating Works

Here's how Riley should have negotiated with the sales force:

"Our expenses are too high. Competitors like Wheelright have lower T&E charges and are underselling us. What can we do about this situation?"

Here, management and sales together would have invented options as part of a negotiation. During the discussions, they would have learned that another contributor to Wheelright's lower prices is that their wheelchair manufacturing is computerized, making the chairs less expensive to produce. Smithson's management would have looked into ways of lowering their own manufacturing costs.

The salespeople would have contacted airlines and hotels and negotiated contracts that would bring them lower prices than even standard fares. The salespeople would have also discovered that, as wheelchair users, they sell the chairs more quickly than their non-disabled counterparts.

The negotiation would have produced a lower cost of goods, lower travel and expense costs, and a greater understanding of the needs and concerns of each side. Rather than going out of business, after using the negotiated strategy Smithson Wheelchairs, Inc. would have had its best year ever.

When You Lose, Nobody Wins

Your other responsibility, as a negotiator, is not to set up deals where you lose and the other side wins. Here's an example:

> Francie has just had a long day when Danielle, a receptionist, asks her late on Thursday if she can take the next day off. Francie's concerned because she's the only other person who knows how to work the switchboard. She has a lot of filing, which she doesn't want to have to do over the weekend. To make things worse, company rules say that vacation time needs to be approved a week in advance.
>
> Francie reluctantly approves the vacation day request, but has to work on Saturday. Her whole day is spent at the filing cabinet cursing Danielle for being irresponsible.

Danielle figured that Francie wouldn't approve her request if it was a bother, so she's totally unaware that Francie's ready to strangle her. By approving the request Francie created a lose–win situation. Lose–win deals usually turn sour quickly. Francie gets even a few days later when her boss asks her who is qualified for a promotion. She tells him:

> "Danielle does good work, but it seems like she's never here. You can't rely on her."

Someone else gets the promotion.

Win–Lose Is One Phase of Five

The first thing to keep in mind when someone comes out with all guns blazing, insisting that they win and that you lose, is that it's the first of five stages (see chapter 6 for details). If you keep responding with reasons why what they're proposing is a win–lose deal, eventually they'll shift conflict resolution styles and become reasonable.

While you're waiting for the next stage to kick in, explain the mutual benefit of a win-win relationship to them. Let's say you're a photographer named Ted and a certain customer, Mandy Chat, is always demanding two-hour service. For her to plan ahead when she needs you to shoot takes a small effort, but she enjoys the power of being able to create a fuss whenever she calls. You're happy to accommodate her occasionally, but now you're finding that she's abusing your generosity. What do you do? Here's an example:

> **TED:** Mandy, we are happy to help you occasionally when you're in a pinch. It seems, though, that the jobs we've been rushing to complete lately have been ones that could have been scheduled.
>
> All our customers are important to us and we're having trouble because these unplanned shoots sometimes cause us to miss deadlines other clients have.

If Mandy says she doesn't care about your other customers, only about her own needs, and if you don't like it then she can find another photographer, you say:

> **TED:** We appreciate the business of all of our customers. The problem is that if everyone made us drop everything for shoots, we couldn't service any of our customers.
> **MANDY:** That's your problem, not mine.

Respond in Terms Others Understand

If Mandy persists, respond in terms she understands.

> **TED:** You sell hair care products, right? Do your customers sometimes need special service?
> **MANDY:** Yes, sometimes they forget to place an order and we have to hustle.
> **TED:** Does that disrupt the shipping staff?
> **MANDY:** Of course it does, but we need to do it, and we expect it of our vendors, too.
> **TED:** Well, we need to be supportive, too. But wouldn't you appreciate it if your customers would follow normal ordering procedure, when they could?
> **MANDY:** Well, yes.

TED: Well, we would too. We're not saying we're not willing to help when we can, but just that we need our customers to plan just like you do.

Mandy is now leaving the win-lose stage and is becoming receptive to collaborative solutions.

MANDY: I see what you mean. I'll tell the marketing people to call you on Mondays to let you know their shooting plans for the week.

TED: That will work. Then we can schedule you and give you all the attention you deserve.

Steps to Handling a Win–Lose Deal

Step 1: Find out their concerns and express your own

Together, invent solutions that work for both of you. Don't filter ideas, consider everything.

Step 2: Write down all the promising ideas

When you're all done, star the ideas that you both think have the best chance of success.

Step 3: Decide, together, which ones are the best

Relationship Management

Relationship management means sustaining long-term win-win alliances. Successful Personality Negotiating begins and ends with your establishing credibility and dealing sincerely with the people you deal with.

Long-Term Relationships Are Complex

Long-term relationships are complex and poor negotiations hurt the relationship, while good negotiations help. During any long-term relationship: business, social, or familial, there will be times when people will become frustrated with each other. Long-term relationships survive because you and others value the relationship. If you occasionally screw up, others will understand. Likewise, cut others slack. It could pay dividends later, and it has the side effect of lowering your blood pressure and making life a lot simpler.

The Tough Questions

Sometimes you have to ask someone a question. You don't want to put them on the spot and you're reluctant to embarrass them, but the issue needs to be addressed. When this happens, follow the lead of ABC's Sam Donaldson, White House reporter for many years.

Sam would use the "Critics of your position would argue . . ." opening to set up his question, and end with "How would you respond to that criticism?" This way Ron or Jimmy or Gerry could deal with the question in an impersonal way. It will work for you, too.

> "Critics of the new time clock say that making managers use it treats them like criminals. How would you respond to that criticism?"

Cognitive Dissonance

People often won't notice mistakes because of a phenomenon called cognitive dissonance. People will be glad they're dealing with you, and successful negotiations themselves will attest that they value the relationship. Cognitive dissonance is when people look for good things about purchases, ideas, plans, and people. It works like this: A family has just spent $2,000 on airfare, parking, hotels, rental cars, etc. for a trip to Orlando, Florida. They would feel like they wasted their money if Disney World was disappointing. They want to feel that visiting Disney World was the best vacation choice they could possibly have made.

So, even if the weather is bad, Mickey Mouse is distracted, and Space Mountain is undergoing repairs, instead of focusing on such disappointments, they'll concentrate on the reasons they had a good time. If another family living in Orlando got free passes and encountered the same situations, you'd hear nothing but complaints. There would be no cognitive dissonance effect, due to the fact the effort to get to the park was negligible and admission was free.

Cognitive dissonance puts people in a positive mind frame. They expect to enjoy Pirates of the Caribbean or Captain Nemo simply because they waited in line for so long to do so. Also, even before they walked down Main Street, America, they were planning to enjoy themselves. That kind of mind-set contributes to how much fun they have because when people plan to like something they usually do.

Sometimes negotiations are complex and take much work. Dissonance works in your favor, especially in long-term relationships, because people want to feel good about the solutions you and they invent. After the negotiation, they'll look for the positive in the agreement.

Could You Do Me a Favor?

Another psychological phenomenon that works for you is that when someone does a favor for you, they are likely to have a more positive feeling toward you. Some people don't want to "put people out" by asking others to do favors for them. Done in moderation, however, people actually like the folks they do things for more than the ones they don't do things for. Why? Many psychologists believe that in doing a favor for someone, we tend to think, "I must like this person, or else I wouldn't be doing anything for them."

Maintaining Stable Relationships

Many people ask what's the best way to guarantee long-term stable relationships. The answer is to reward constructive behavior with constructive behavior and punish destructive behavior with destructive behavior.

This strategy is based on a system called "tit for tat" developed by Professor Anatol Rapaport of the University of Toronto for a competition held by Robert Axelrod.[2] The competition was to see who could find the best solution to a negotiation seminar standard, "The Prisoner's Dilemma."

The Prisoner's Dilemma Game

"The Prisoner's Dilemma" is a game played by two people. Each, hypothetically, has been arrested for a crime and faces the possibility of a long jail term. Either prisoner, while alone, can confess against the other. This is seemingly in his best interest since the confessor will be released and the other prisoner will be guaranteed the full jail term.

However, if both prisoners squeal then both will get the full sentence. Finally, if both cooperate (with each other, not the police) then they'll be convicted on a minor charge and serve only a short sentence.

The game involves a set number of rounds, and instead of sending the players to jail, they get points based on the outcome. The idea is to amass as many points as possible. For cooperation both get three points. For confessing they get five points if their partner is silent, but no points if both confess or if the partner confesses.

	Player B cooperates	Player B confesses
Player A cooperates	A gets 3 B gets 3	A gets 0 B gets 5
Player A confesses	A gets 5 B gets 0	A gets 0 B gets 0

Rapaport's solution is a predominantly cooperative method that works well for all types of negotiation. In fact, his strategy amassed *by far* the largest number of points in multiple round of play.

The way it works is this: you begin by being cooperative. From that point on you return a "nice" move for a "nice" move and a selfish move for a selfish move, that is, tit for tat.

The key to the success of tit for tat is that you are mercilessly selfish until the other side is cooperative, then you become immediately cooperative. Rapaport's tit for tat solution, according to negotiation expert Susan Heitler,[3] works for several reasons:

1. **It works with a variety of personality types and conflict resolution styles.** People of all types recognize intuitively when others are acting cooperatively or selfishly, so interpretation is easy.
2. **It reinforces ongoing relationships.** Acting selfishly can have short-term gains for one and short-term losses for another. Tit for tat optimizes the gain for both parties.
3. **Niceness pays.** Relationships that begin with benevolence itself usually put people in a cooperative mood. You don't have to worry that being nice too soon will hurt your negotiation stance.
4. **Selfishness costs.** "The Prisoner's Dilemma," like most negotiations, frequently begins with cooperation, which erodes when one party lets selfishness take over and tries to maximize personal gain. In tit for tat, it is quickly apparent that cooperation is more lucrative than selfishness.
5. **Pessimism costs.** People who are selfishly defensive, assuming the other side is out to get them, learn that they gain much more by trust.
6. **It is highly responsive.** Negotiators see that alterations in their behavior are met immediately with positive or negative consequences. This, too, adds to stability.

Since tit for tat was developed in 1984, negotiators have successfully used it in a variety of situations. It maximizes gain and promotes long-term bonds.

Sow the Seeds Early—Then React

Another key ingredient to holding on to a relationship is to recognize when people aren't happy and do something about it as soon as you can. Remember that some people, especially Feeling types, are likely to keep their emotions bottled up inside them. They play, "read my mind." The read-my-mind game works like this. One person is unhappy for some reason, but doesn't say anything. It's up to the other people playing the game to figure it out.

Since people aren't mind readers, they usually lose the game. Sadly, "read my mind" is the biggest cause of negotiation breakdown.

The way you stop "read my mind" is to express your thoughts. Instead of hoping others will figure out what you are thinking, assume that they won't—which is usually the case.

To keep "read my mind" from destroying your negotiations, use your version of the following. Early in any relationship, ask the people you're dealing with to let you know whenever they're unhappy or have concerns:

> "I'm going to try my best to address your concerns. Anytime something disturbs you, let me know, so I can address that issue. Sometimes people don't tell others their concerns and hope that others can figure out what's bothering them without saying anything. I can't read your mind, and you can't read mine. Two-way communication is essential."

Giving people "permission" to tell you they're not happy allows them to express their feelings. It allows you to focus on issues before the issues become serious. We all know that the earlier we know about a problem or concern the easier it is to deal with it.

Allow People to Vent Their Emotions

If the people you're dealing with are agitated, allow them to vent their emotions. If things get out of hand, very gently say, hold on. Use the same tactics you would use with the Exploder (in chapter 12).

If you're dealing with Introverts, they might have some unspoken concerns and complaints that they keep bottled up until they're asked. If you allow them to express their concerns, they'll be glad that you provided them the chance to have someone listen to them. There will still be issues to deal with, but you'll be communicating.

If Introverts get cut off before they're done expressing their thoughts, their frustrations will be locked inside them, and the relationship is doomed.

If you're dealing with Extroverts, they may tend to get off track. Concentrate on the issues and make sure that the negotiation stays on track.

Short-Term Negotiations

If you have an ending relationship, negotiation can be tricky. On the one hand, you may never be seeing or hearing from the person again. On the other hand, you never know. All the principles of long-term negotiation still apply. You'll still do better with a collaborative solution than a win-lose one.

Another critical part of short-term negotiations is the effect they have on third-party observers. If one party acts unreasonably towards someone with the thought, "who cares, I'll never see them again," it's true, they *may* never see *that* person again—but could have daily contact with the people observing the interaction.

> Rick Jameson was just appointed president of a medium-sized company. Rick had learned, at a prestigious university, that the first thing one should do as president is fire a few people.
>
> Even though she was a top employee, he decided to fire Lisa, who happened to be married to a wealthy trial lawyer.

Rick felt good about his decision, especially since Lisa, a conflict avoider, persuaded her husband not to sue. Because of the unwarranted firing, others in the company saw Rick as a tyrant and never trusted him.

Even years later, people thought of Rick as a skilled manipulator, and he never got the valuable support he could have had from his employees. He constantly had to interact with other members of the company who thought, "Sure he's dealt fairly with me so far, but how long will it be until I get fired, despite the fact that I'm a good worker?"

When you're involved in short-term negotiations, remember that how you handle yourself will live long after the short-term relationship has ended.

The next chapter deals with a special kind of negotiations—negotiating with salespeople.

Conclusion

The only deals that will work long-term are deals in which both parties win. Make sure that every deal you enter is win-win. Taking people for a ride or letting others take advantage of you will ultimately spiral the relationship to a lose-lose one. Match constructive behavior with constructive behavior and destructive behavior with destructive behavior. Follow these steps to be a consultative negotiator:

STEP 1: Discover your and others' concerns.
STEP 2: Find areas of common interest.
STEP 3: Tell others that you want a win-win deal.

When you're inventing ideas, use these steps:

STEP 1: Write down all the promising ideas.
STEP 2: Decide together which ones are the best.

Remember that negotiations can take on lives of their own, and short-term negotiations are no exception.

NOTES

1. Claude M. Steiner, *Scripts People Live* (New York: Bantam Books, 1975), 253–267.
2. Robert Axelrod, *The Evolution of Cooperation* (New York: Basic Books, 1984).
3. Heitler, *From Conflict to Resolution*, 13–15.

Chapter 10
NEGOTIATING WITH SALESPEOPLE

Negotiating with salespeople is different from most negotiations. As the customer, you're the ultimate decision maker. Salespeople, too, have power. They know the cost of the goods you buy and control the delivery of a product or service you need. Before you enter into a sales negotiation with a salesperson you don't know, beware—but don't be defensive. Remember that most salespeople are honest and will try to help you fill your needs at a fair price. But there are other types of salespeople—some have learned how to manipulate buyers. They are often successful in coaxing shoppers to buy things they don't need at exorbitant prices.

Charlatan salespeople are in the minority. This chapter covers specific strategies for dealing with this type of unscrupulous salesperson and explains why there aren't many of them.

Since honest salespeople are the norm, let's look at how to deal with them, first.

The First Sale Is Expensive

The first sale a salesperson makes to you takes the most effort—by far. Highly-paid salespeople become highly paid because customers regularly buy from them and refer their friends to them. They strive for referral sales that are easy money and require little effort. For example, Harry, at Quick Printers, has been dealing with Jim for several years. Whenever Jim hears that someone is looking for a printer, the following occurs.

> "I've been dealing with Harry at Quick Printers for five years now, and he gets all my business. Give Harry a call. He's dependable, provides great service, and really knows what he's doing."

Jim's endorsement is typical of the millions of conversations that take place every day when satisfied customers act as ad agencies for salespeople who have treated them right. Salespeople need customers to refer their friends and colleagues to them, so most will be eager to work with you as best they can. Disenchanted customers, however, are a much different story.

Unhappy Customers Stay Away

Customers who get gypped don't come back, and they certainly don't give out referrals. Eventually, the dishonest salespeople are pushed out of the sales force. They can't survive if all their sales are the time-consuming and expensive first sales, with none of the easy repeat sales to pad their stats. They simply don't make enough money to stay in sales, so they find another line of work. Their underhanded tactics act as a kind of population control for sales forces.

The next section looks at what to expect when you buy from an on-the-level salesperson. Even when the salesperson is not a con-artist, many of us dread spending money because we feel that we are at a disadvantage. This section takes the mystery out of shopping.

Sales Negotiations

Many people don't realize it, but they tend to follow a predictable pattern when they buy. Salespeople know this and respond by selling in a very methodical manner. Also, people naturally tend to seek out salespeople who are similar to them in personality type. Personality Selling, Personality Negotiating's companion for salespeople, works because salespeople adapt the way they sell to the way customers want to buy. This makes negotiation easier for both customer and rep.

If your salesperson isn't using Personality Selling, you take the reins and control the sale. Using Personality Negotiating, you'll know what to expect in the sales cycle and can train the salesperson to adapt to your preferences using your knowledge of personality type. The negotiation will be smooth and the results fruitful. Instead of being in a weak negotiating position, you'll be in a strong one. Although each salesperson and each company is different, you can expect the following sequence to occur during a sales negotiation:

Step 1: You and Salesperson Make Contact

Sometimes you find the salesperson, perhaps through the Yellow Pages. Sometimes the salesperson contacts you. This contact could be indirect, through an ad or a mass-mailing piece; or direct, by telephone or in-person.

Based on your personality type, you'll have a favorite way of being contacted by salespeople. Most salespeople, being Extroverts, will prefer to set up an in-person meeting to begin negotiations. Extroverted customers prefer in-person meetings as well, and if that's best for you, great. Introverted customers tend to like to receive written information and conduct negotiations by telephone. If that's your preference, let the salesperson know.

> **DON:** I'd prefer you send me the specs in the mail. This will give me a chance to analyze them when I'm not distracted.

Many salespeople are taught that if customers say they want to analyze quotations privately, what that really means is they're getting the old kiss-off. So, sales reps will likely push for a meeting. If you don't want a meeting, don't be pressured into one. Instead, educate the salesperson by saying that, although you don't want to meet, you are interested in dealing with him or her.

> **RICH:** Though I want you to send me the background literature, don't take that to mean I don't want to deal with you. I do. I'm very busy now and a meeting would be a waste of your time and mine.
>
> I get the best grasp of the data you send me when I can analyze it with no distractions. The best time for me is early in the morning, when I'm alone in the office.
>
> When I'm ready for a meeting, I'll let you know.

Step 2: You Both Gather Information

This is the part of the negotiation where you both decide if a business relationship is mutually beneficial.

You're going to want to know about the salesperson's experience and the company's reputation. Most salespeople will volunteer this. If they don't, then ask.

> "What experience have you had in dealing with companies like mine?"

Salespeople are going to want to know about your purchasing history, purchasing plans, and requirements. If they don't ask you what you like and dislike about your current product, method, or vendor, let them know. This will help them keep what you like and change what you don't like.

If you think they don't completely understand your needs, volunteer more about what you want. This will make the rest of the negotiation go smoothly.

Step 3: A Proposal Is Made

The next step is for the salesperson to give you a quotation. The elaborateness of the proposal will be proportional to how much you are spending. If you're buying one computer, it's likely to consist of a review of your needs and a one-page cost breakdown of your system's components. If you're buying a thousand computers, it is likely to be a multimedia event held at their expense in Honolulu.

If the salesperson understood you during the information-gathering stage, the quote is likely to be very close to what your expressed needs were. If the pricing or components are way off, there was a communication lapse somewhere. More information gathering is needed.

Step 4: Salesperson Asks for Your Response

After the salesperson makes the offer he or she will want to know what you think about it. Expect open-ended questions (questions that need more than a one-word answer) like, "What do you think about the proposal?" Open-ended questions give the salesperson valuable feedback that allows modifications or "tweaking" to make the purchase perfect for you.

If you get a closed-ended question, one you can answer only in one word, and you feel that the salesperson needs more to go on, expand.

> **SALESPERSON:** I think this reflects what we discussed, don't you?
> **CUSTOMER:** Yes. I like what you sent me, generally, but I wouldn't accept it in its current form because it doesn't mention delivery dates.

Step 5: Salesperson Tries to Wrap Up Deal

If the proposal meets your needs, salespeople will want you to accept it, and will attempt a trial close. (This is similar to the trial close negotiators use. Its function is not to get a commitment, but to force a response—see chapter 5.) They'll ask you to wrap up the deal, knowing that you might not be ready, by saying things like, "Does this color match your furniture?" or "I'll check to see if any are in stock."

Salespeople know that your liking the proposal is one thing, but your spending money is another. If you come back with responses like, "It will look great with my wallpaper," or "What days do you deliver?" they know you are ready to close.

If you're not ready to buy, you'll be inclined to say, "I think that question's a little premature," or "Don't waste your time checking on inventory."

Trial balloons are an important part of sales (or any type of negotiation). These questions force you to think hard about what you're buying, and what your needs really are.

Almost always there are last-minute issues that crop up once you're faced with writing a check or purchase order. Now's the time to address these issues. Speak up, because after you've bought, it may be too late.

Step 6: Rep Tries to Close the Sale

If you're both coming out winners, then buying should be a pleasant experience—you've just bought something that you need at a fair price. (Of course, buying a big-screen TV is a lot more pleasant than buying a refrigerator!) At this point in the sales cycle, you'll notice the rep asking closed-ended questions. He wants you to get used to saying yes. (He also wants to make sure he's addressed all your points.) He'll say things like:

> **REP:** Does what I'm proposing answer all your needs?
> **CUSTOMER:** Yes.
> **REP:** Is the price we've arrived at in your budget?
> **CUSTOMER:** Yes.
> **REP:** Do we have a deal?
> **CUSTOMER:** Yes.

Step 7: Delivery and After-the-Sale Support

The final part of the sales cycle is the delivery of your purchase and the after-the-sale support. Soon after you've made the purchase, the salesperson will receive commission money. Commissions vary, but they're usually around five to fifteen percent of the sale. Salespeople don't make any money from after-the-sale support, but they hope that their efforts will lead you to buy from them again and to recommend them to your friends. You paid for support as part of the price of what you bought. You deserve it, so insist on it when you need it.

You deserve a high level of support from your salesperson. The salesperson can usually answer questions to typical problems. For example, if you have just bought a VCR and can't figure out the cabling from the instructions, call the salesperson who sold it to you. Chances are that other customers have had the same problem and the salesperson will be able to help you instantly.

Other more complex questions may need some research. Salespeople often have access to technical knowledge at work or through special answer-line numbers manufacturers provide their customers that aren't available to the public. If you are hooking a VCR up to a multi-unit entertainment system, the salesperson may not know what fits where off the top of his or her head—give the salesperson a reasonable amount of time to solve complex problems.

Never, never accept, "Sorry, since you didn't buy the TV from me, I can't help you." You bought a functioning VCR, not a hunk of electronics in a box—insist that it functions.

Insist Nicely

If you're not getting the service that you paid for, then insist on it. Implicit or explicit in your negotiation with the salesperson was the promise that what you're buying fills your needs and functions correctly. You have the right to expect that salespeople, or anyone, keep to agreements made during a negotiation.

When exercising your rights, maintain assertiveness and persevere. Use the same negotiating skills now that you would use anywhere: educate the salesperson, ask sincere questions, deal with them according to personality type, work out collaborative solutions and, especially if you are getting the runaround, separate the person from the problem.

Focusing all your efforts on the salesperson makes him or her the problem, not what you need to have accomplished. If the salesperson is being difficult, then deal with that issue later. Here's a succession of strategies to use to get what you deserve.

Nancy took off her lunch hour to return to the VCR store to ask Al, the salesperson, how to get a VCR she had bought the night before to work:

> **NANCY:** Good afternoon. This VCR I bought last night isn't working. Could you show me what I might be doing wrong?
> **AL:** Sure, I'll be with you as soon as I finish with this customer.

After finishing with that customer, instead of going to Nancy, he avoids her and approaches someone who looks as if he's about to buy. This annoys Nancy, but instead of getting angry, she asserts herself. Her tone and attitude are still very pleasant toward the salesperson. This way, the VCR, not the salesperson, remains the problem.

> **NANCY:** (To Al) Here I am. (To the other customer) Al was looking for me so he could explain how to run the VCR I bought last night. I'm on my lunch hour, and I have to hurry. Look, that salesperson over there's free. I'm sure she'll be happy to take your order. (To Al) Where were we? Oh, yes. The VCR doesn't work.

Nancy's not being aggressive. Al had said that he would help her next, and she's seeing that that happens. Nancy doesn't try to diagnose the VCR problem herself. That's not her job, it's Al's.

> **AL:** I think the problem is the way you're hooking up the cables. Keep trying, it will work.
>
> **NANCY:** I tried every conceivable combination, and none of them worked. (Nancy is explaining her concerns.)
>
> **AL:** Sorry, I can't help you. Why don't you try the store where you bought the TV?
>
> **NANCY:** Because I spent $350 for a VCR bought from here last night. One of the reasons I bought this model was the promise that it would work with my TV. (Very pleasantly.) So, how does it work with my TV?

Nancy certainly deserves to be furious with Al. Still, hostility on her part will only create hostility on his part. Despite Al's uncooperativeness, Nancy perseveres in keeping Al separate from the problem of the VCR's not working.

> **AL:** Sorry, I can't help you.
>
> **NANCY:** You may not know how to hook up the cable, but you can certainly help me. Why don't you call the manufacturer? Maybe they could help. (Nancy is exploring alternatives.)
>
> **AL:** That could take a long time, and I'm real busy at lunch time. (Al knows that people use their lunch hours to browse and to buy. He is worried that other salespeople will take orders while he's on the phone. Ironically, Nancy is a Feeling-type customer and would have tried to work with Al, even if it meant a little inconvenience, if Al hadn't tried to brush her off earlier.)
>
> **NANCY:** What do you mean by a long time? (Nancy is doing information gathering.)
>
> **AL:** It could take as much as forty-five minutes.
>
> **NANCY:** That's fine. I'll leave the VCR here, get some lunch, and come back. (To make sure the phone call happens) I'll wait until you make contact with the manufacturer, in case they have any questions.

It turns out that the call doesn't take forty-five minutes, only ten, but the manufacturer's suggestion was only that Nancy follow the directions in the manual. Nancy knows that she has tried every cabling combination possible.

AL: Sorry, there's nothing we can do.

NANCY: That may be true. However, my concern is still that I paid top dollar for a VCR that claims to work with every TV. Returning the unit would be a losing deal for you, and I like this unit, so having to find another would be a losing deal for me, too. (Explanation of everyone's concerns.) What if I hire a professional installer and send you the bill? (Advancing a collaborative solution.)

AL: I'm sorry, that's against company policy.

NANCY: If the unit doesn't connect to my TV, it is useless to me. Before I return it, check to see if someone can override company policy and pay for the installation.

Al, who doesn't want to lose the sale, talks with his boss, Joan. Joan talks with Nancy regarding her suggestion and recognizes the fact that the loss of money on the return and the bad will created by Al are not worth the relatively small installation charge involved. Joan calls an installer whom the store uses and sets up an installation for that evening.

With the installation problem addressed, Nancy turns to the problem of Al's lack of customer service. She tells Joan that if Nancy's company treated its customers the way Al treated theirs, Nancy's company would be out of business. (That evening, the installer found that Nancy's cable company used a box that needed a special adaptor not included with the VCR. It was impossible for Nancy to get the unit working without that piece.)

Should Nancy decide to buy a second VCR for upstairs, the sale will be easier and she'll need less support because she'll know to purchase the needed adaptor also. Generally, the second sale is more straightforward for everyone.

You Get Benefits from that Second Sale

Since repeat sales become increasingly cheaper for your salesperson, he or she will benefit from maintaining a relationship. And so should you. You'll find that you get better service, more accommodating conditions, and often a lower price when you're a regular customer.

> Helen is Kitchen Magic's best customer. They know the types of gadgets she likes to buy, and call her when they're having a sale on them. If she can't buy during that sale, they put the item on layaway for her.

The more you buy, the more valuable you are as a customer. If you're a regular customer with a big budget, like a purchasing agent, most companies will plan expansion and inventory around your purchases.

Sometimes suppliers start cruising on reputation and take your business for granted, creating a Lose–Win deal with you losing. Don't allow this to happen. Every relationship is marked by hills and valleys, so before cutting off your vendors, try to work with them. By staying with them you'll not only keep the benefits of a long-term buying relationship, but earn vast amounts of goodwill by sticking by them when you didn't have to. This goodwill could be valuable down the road.

> Last year, First Bank bought a million dollars in ATM's from O'Leary's Financial Sales. Since First Bank was O'Leary's best customer they got outstanding pricing and service.
>
> This year, First Bank's purchases have slowed because of the economy. Since First Bank has developed much goodwill, O'Leary's will continue to give them their best service.
>
> In return, when business picks up at First Bank, O'Leary's will get all of First Bank's ATM business.

Here are some specific strategies for using Personality Negotiating to deal with salespeople.

Deal with Salespeople You Know or Stores You Trust

Salespeople you've dealt with before aren't going to want to lose you as a customer. They won't want to kill the goose that lays the golden egg by taking advantage of you. If you've been referred, the same thing applies, except the goose is the friend or colleague who referred you.

> Mary is the purchasing agent for one of The Computer Market's biggest customers. If you tell the salesperson that Mary referred you when you buy your single computer, you'll get the same treatment Mary would get. If you get taken, they'll lose Mary's business.

Expect a Lot of Questions

Good salespeople know they can't help you until they understand your needs. Tell them as much as makes you comfortable. Remember, the more data they have, the better the solution they can devise. Educate the salesperson on what is significant to you. If you're a Sensing-type person, then practicality will be important to you. If you're a Feeling type person, a consideration that needs addressing will be the benefit others will receive from the product or service you're buying. Make sure the sales rep understands this.

> **THINKING-TYPE SALES REP:** I know that this fax machine seems hard to use at first, but they'll figure out how to use it eventually.
> **FEELING-TYPE CUSTOMER:** We've never had a fax machine. If it's hard to operate, then my employees wouldn't use it. They might resent having it in the office.

Usually, educating salespeople is effective because they want to make the sale. Even if they don't appreciate your concerns, they'll keep offering solutions until they've hit on the one that suits you. Buying something that isn't right for you is a Win-Lose deal, and Win-Lose deals should always be avoided. Instead of settling for something you know isn't working, insist that effort be put into making the solution right:

> **FEELING-TYPE CUSTOMER:** While it may be unimportant to you that the fax machine be easy to operate, it's very important to me. Since you don't want me to buy a machine from someone else, let's explore other alternatives.

Flexing your muscles is a very powerful force that you, as the customer, have at your disposal. While flexing, keep in mind that you want the sales rep to win, too.

Make Sales Rep Let You Speak

Sometimes customers can't get a word in edgewise because the rep is talking so much. Considering that the vast majority of salespeople are Extroverts, this isn't surprising. If you're an Introvert, train the salesperson to be quiet while you think. Telling them "Hold on for a few seconds" usually does the trick. Remember, Extroverts measure times of silence much differently than Introverts do. Ten seconds of pondering time may seem short to an Introvert, but an Extrovert may have an uncontrollable urge to fill that time by saying *some*thing. So, if you're an Introvert, keep in mind that your notion of "a few seconds" is likely to be much different from an Extrovert's.

Don't Be Rushed into a Decision

There are few things more frustrating than making a purchase, and then lamenting over it because you made it too quickly. Almost all salespeople are Judging types. This means that they'll try to get you to set dates and times for making decisions. If you're a Perceiving-type person you are likely to make decisions only when your criteria are met, despite timetables. Make sure you decide when it is comfortable for *you*, not for the salesperson:

> "I'll buy when my buying criteria are met. I'll get the doughnut maker when I'm convinced it can make 2,000 doughnuts a day and won't be broken for more than two hours at a time. If there's one Sunday morning when I can't serve doughnuts because of an equipment failure, I'll lose many of my customers.
>
> If you can show me that your product does what I need today, I'll buy today. If you show me that three months from now, I'll buy three months from now.

If you, like the salesperson, are Judging type, don't let the reinforcement of sharing the same personality preference hinder your negotiation. Both you and the Judging-type salesperson are going to find coming to closure very natural, but that closure may be premature. Be alert to it.

> **MICHELLE:** By tomorrow, I want to make a decision on which siding to get for the house, but I'm not thrilled with your selection.
> **SALESPERSON:** If you want to get the siding installed in four days, on Saturday, you'll have to order it today.
> **MICHELLE:** I guess what you have will have to do.

If you're faced with this type of situation in a negotiation, what you need to do is decide whether the deadline is real or artificial. Play out the worst-case scenario in your mind. Will siding installation after Saturday have severe negative consequences? Are the negative effects of deciding worse than those associated with not deciding? If so, continue to explore alternatives.

> **MICHELLE:** I wanted to decide now, but I'm just not comfortable with my choices. I'll wait, because I don't want to look at an ugly color for years to come.

The negotiation now consists of Michelle and her salesperson discovering alternatives, covered in chapter 6. The next section gives you specific strategies for maneuvering in the negotiation.

Negotiating Price

Negotiating a lower price is a terrible experience for many people. In fact, most consumers hate the whole process and when it's done, worry that they did not negotiate very well.

> Valerie is having a yard sale and wants to sell her gas grill. She has it marked at $80, but would be thrilled to get $50 for it.
>
> Steve is in the market for a gas grill. New grills sell for $200 so if he could get a good used grill for $80, he'd take it, but he'd pay as much as $100.
>
> When Steve gets to the yard sale and sees the grill for $80, he buys it immediately. This is a classic Win-Win deal. Both feel they have won because they got the deal that they wanted.
>
> As Steve is leaving, he tells Valerie, "What a great deal! I would have spent $100 for this grill."
>
> Then Valerie confesses, "I would have taken $50 for it."
>
> Both Steve and Valerie now wish they had more money in their pockets, and are dissatisfied with the deal they negotiated.

Actually, both Valerie and Steve should be happy because they each got what they wanted. It's not the price of the grill that disturbs them, it's the lingering feeling that each could have done better.

You Did Fine

If the grill you want is $80 and you get it for $80 then relax, you did well. Good sales negotiations wind up with fair prices—if the price is fair, the negotiation was a success.

Many negotiations focus solely on price, and that's unfortunate. Price is only one part of a successful purchase, and there's no such thing as a free lunch. If you pay more, you'll usually get better service. Companies that charge too little go out of business, and then you're left with no service at all.

Take the entire package into consideration when you negotiate and you'll come out with a good balance of quality, price, service, and company reputation. Still, there are techniques you can use to help you get a fair price.

Do Your Homework

Get as many statistics as you can about the dealer price and average retail selling price of what you're buying. If you're buying a car, *Consumer Reports*, AAA, credit unions, and many other sources have complete data on the dealer cost of every car and option. These publications also tell you the average retail and selling prices of the cars you're considering.

> **BUYER:** The retail price of the model I'm interested in is $11,000, and your cost is $6,000. According to *Consumer Reports*, the average purchase price is $8,351. That price would give you a fair profit and me a fair discount. I'd be happy to give you a check right now for that amount.
> **SALESPERSON:** Sold.

In today's computer age, this type of data is available on almost any product. If you don't know where to find it, ask the reference librarian at your local library to help find the resources for you.

Once you've bought your product, and the salesperson is trying to sell you accessories, called add-ons, knowing about margins is most helpful.

Add-ons Bring in the Margins

Margin is sales talk for the markup of a product. Gillette gives away (sells without profit) the handles to their razors so they can sell the blades that fit them. Track II handles only work with Track II blades, which have a very high profit margin. Other high margin add-ons include printer ribbons, computer disks, video tapes, furniture polish, six-way adjustable mirrors for cars, and service contracts.

Add-on margins are key for you, as the consumer, to be aware of in that you'll find that salespeople will try to inflate the size of the sale with add-ons after you've bought the main product.

In retail sales, it's common for no money to be made on the basic product, and all the profit to be made on the add-ons.

> Computer printers are made by many companies and the discounting is typically extremely high. The computer store breaks even on the printers they sell. However, they make almost pure profit on the 20 percent per year maintenance of

the product. If they take in $1,000 in maintenance money, they'll use about $200 for commissions, $200 for fixing printers, and keep the rest.

Other types of add-ons are stain-proofing your upholstered furniture, telephoto lenses, vacuum-cleaner bags, gadget bags for your camera, rust-proofing your car, and extra supplies of batteries.

The most common type of add-on is a maintenance contract. Depending on the product, maintenance can be a very good, or a very bad deal for you.

Buying Maintenance Can Be a Win–Win Deal

Buying maintenance contracts can be a Win–Win deal depending on the price of the contract and the cost of replacement. For instance, if you could get a complete support contract for your car at $200, that would be an offer you couldn't refuse.

If someone offered you a $200 per year contract on a color TV that cost $350 to replace, that would be an offer you wouldn't take.

Maintenance is a kind of insurance policy. Since everyone is comfortable with different levels of risk, the benefits of maintenance contracts are unique to each person.

> Publishers are wise to buy expensive maintenance contracts for their overworked Xerox copiers, while a company that makes five or ten copies a day would be foolish to buy the same contract.

If you feel the terms of the contract are not in your favor, negotiate a better deal. Maintenance on items that rarely break are pure profit for the vendor. If there is fat in the contract, your salesperson will have room to negotiate a deal that benefits both of you.

Another type of salesmanship is used by the type of salesperson who is trying to con you or pressure you into buying something you'll regret. The next section shows you how to spot and deal with these sales reps.

Don't Go For Gimmicks

There are lots of gimmicks salespeople have dreamed up over the years. Most of them have their roots in history, as far back as ancient Rome. One of the more popular scams is called good cop/bad cop. (In ancient

Rome it was called good centurion/bad centurion.) It works like this: Jerry and Rita have just completed the negotiation for a car with their salesperson, Ralph. After they sign the contract, Ralph, the good cop, tells them that he can't authorize any sale other than list-price sales and must get approval from his boss.

> **RALPH:** (upon returning) That jerk of a boss. (the bad cop) He wouldn't take it. I told him how much you needed the car, but he said I went $500 too low. I fought for you, but he won't budge.

In the time Ralph and his boss were "arguing," they were hoping that Jerry and Rita would take psychological ownership of the car and buy it under any circumstances. The technical term for this phenomenon is cognitive dissonance, or ignoring negative evidence about things that you like or want. Most customers would tell Ralph to stick it sideways, but some will, as Ralph hopes, pay another $500.

No matter what they say, Ralph and his manager are not adversaries. They have common goals, share commissions, and are working together. If a salesperson tells you differently, know he or she is trying to con you.

There Is Always Tomorrow

Usually people have a gut instinct for sleazy salespeople that's on target. Go with your instinct. There is never any once-in-a-lifetime deal, or a similar one, that can't be found tomorrow. If a salesperson pressures you into acting immediately, walk away from the negotiation.

> **SLEAZY SALESPERSON:** After touring the health club, I'm sure you can appreciate the excellent facilities. There is an initiation fee of $500. If you sign up before you leave, that fee will only be $300, but when you walk out that door, it will be $200 more. (Sometimes they will valet-park your car, and delay giving you the keys for hours until you sign up.)
> **SAVVY CUSTOMER:** I'm not going to sign up today, and if I decide to join, I'll only pay $300. Pressuring me any more will just convince me never to return. (If you don't give me my keys, I'll call the police.)

What dishonest salespeople know is that if you sleep on the deal you'll realize that it's not in your best interest, and won't come back. Any deal worth making is worth making next week. If you have doubts, hold off.

If You Get Taken

If you get taken, don't panic. Most states allow a short time to get a full refund on any purchase—usually forty-eight or seventy-two hours. Call your state's Consumer Affairs office for your specific rights.

There is an implied warranty in all products that the product will serve its intended purpose. If you feel you have a lemon, and have not been able to get satisfaction from the seller or manufacturer, call your Consumer Affairs office for their help and input and reopen negotiations. As a last resort, see an attorney about the procedures you need to negotiate a return of costs legally.

Conclusion

When you're involved in a sales negotiation, both you and the salesperson have power. You have the power to purchase, and he has the power to withhold something you need. Salespeople also know the cost of what you want and may be experienced at manipulating you.

If the salesperson isn't interested in a Win-Win deal, then it's up to you to teach him how to deal with you. Expect your salesperson to ask you questions to find your needs and to check your reaction to his offers. If the offer is good, take it. If the offer isn't, give your reasons for refusal and work towards a better deal.

Finally, be watchful for scam artists and avoid them.

Chapter 11
SPOTTING AND COUNTERING NEGOTIATION TRAPS

One of the things many negotiators fear is falling for sleazy tactics and coming out of the negotiation having been taken.

A most frustrating element in negotiations is hearing statements that sound okay initially but, once analyzed, don't make sense. Negotiators may know something's fishy, but aren't able to pick up on the problem with the reasoning so can't respond as well as they would like. The cause is verbal trickery, and it's been around for thousands of years. In this chapter, we'll use a modern-day version of the ancient Greek art of rhetoric to combat the fallacious reasoning.

Coming up, you'll learn how to spot the top twenty fallacious arguments used in negotiations and proven strategies for responding to them effectively.

Negotiation Tactics

Sometimes people will pretend to negotiate, but they are really battling. If you'd be better off without a deal than with the negotiated one, then don't accept it. As the saying goes, "Sometimes the best deals you make are the ones you walk away from."

The best way not to get taken is to know your bottom line well before the negotiation begins so you won't get swept up in the heat of battle and agree to something you'll regret later. This is covered in detail in chapter 2. Here is one tactic often used in negotiations:

Confusing the Issue
Confusing the issue is used, for example, when a drawback is substantive, but the matter is treated as inconsequential.

> **UNSCRUPULOUS SALESPERSON:** Don't worry that the chair's a little scratched. It'll get scratched in your kitchen, anyway.

CUSTOMER: Get me a new chair.

The key to good negotiation is listening. Good negotiators tend to be good listeners. Hone those skills, and use them during negotiations. You'll wind up with deals in which all parties get what they want.

Catching People in Verbal Trickery

When certain arguments appear to sound fine, but they leave a lingering feeling that something isn't right, it's the result of verbal trickery, or faulty reasoning.[1] The strategy of verbal trickery is to catch you off guard and pressure you into a decision while you're still unsure about the arguments. This type of negotiation works because the flaws of the arguments are well-disguised and sound convincing.

Here are some examples of verbal trickery and on-the-ball responses:

BREAKING THE CAMEL'S BACK: Assuming small amounts are unimportant.

> **SALESPERSON:** You can rent this personal computer during the school year for only $30 a week.
> **STUDENT:** (focusing on the total amount) I'd be paying almost $4,000 to rent a system to use during college that I could buy for $1,000.

This reasoning also comes up in reverse—putting too much emphasis on small amounts.

> **VIDEO STORE AD:** Rent movies now! Bargain prices— slashed 10%.
> **CUSTOMER:** (thinking) The $3 cost only drops 30¢. Instead of spending $2.70 here, I can rent the same movie at the supermarket for 99¢.

ARGUING IN A CIRCLE: This happens when conclusions get stated as arguments.

> **CEO:** Statistics in our annual report show that we are the industry leader.
> **STOCKBROKER:** What you're saying is that you're the industry leader because you say you're the industry leader. Anyone can make claims about themselves. The claims must be substantiated by other proof.

LOGICAL LEAP: A logical leap happens when people try to get others to draw conclusions without supporting evidence.

PRESIDENT: Our workers have excellent productivity. They must think highly of the company.

UNION NEGOTIATOR: There's no relation between productivity and liking the company. Productive employees aren't necessarily happy ones.

LOADED STATEMENT: A loaded statement is a conclusion presented as fact. The person then builds upon that "fact," often with correct reasoning.

RESTAURATEUR: We have done more business over the years because of our steadfast commitment to quality, service, and value.

There are two loaded statements here. The first is whether, in fact, more business has been done, and secondly, whether the reasons are the commitments to quality, etc.

BANKER: What do you mean by "more business," and are you sure it isn't because of some other variables—like you've been the only restaurant in town?

PERSONAL ATTACK: This is when you're attacked personally for something unrelated to the issue being discussed.

EXPERIENCED MANAGER: You're still wet behind the ears—you can take all the college courses you want—it doesn't mean you know squat.

NEWLY HIRED MANAGER: The issue here isn't age, but expertise. I'm fully knowledgeable about the areas we're discussing.

SYMPATHY GRABBING: This occurs when people attempt to sway with pity.

JERRY: If Mike moves to the accounting office, I won't have anyone to play racquetball with anymore.

ACCOUNTING MANAGER: I feel badly that you and Mike can't play racquetball at lunchtime, but we need him in accounting.

QUESTIONABLE SOURCES: Questionable sources include non-experts, experts in one field giving opinions in another area, or things people may have read.

"Oliver North says this is the finest baseball glove in the world."

"What are North's qualifications for making such an endorsement? Only a baseball player can make such a claim."

"Barbra Streisand says that the new Buick is the best car built."

"Streisand may know about movies, but that doesn't mean she knows about cars."

"I read someplace that their product is very expensive to repair."

"Until we know what the article said, and in which magazine, we can't make any conclusions about the statement's validity."

BUILDING A STRAW MAN (also straw dog): A straw man is built by falsely exaggerating the importance of side issues and then attacking them as if they were the main issue. This tends to take the focus off real issues that are not easily attacked. (A straw man will blow down in the wind.)

Here is what happens when a textile company dumping sewage into a river in northern New Hampshire is opposed by a local environmentalist group trying to stop the practice. Denise McCarthy, Vice President of Operations at the company tells reporters:

> **McCARTHY:** Environmental groups are nothing but a bunch of people with nothing better to do. In a recent article, which I show you now, a group located in Los Angeles suggested that we bury our cars so the ice caps won't melt. Without cars, people wouldn't be able to get to work, and the automobile industry would be ruined.

McCarthy tries to divert attention away from the problem of sewage to: 1) the doings of some extremist environmental group, and 2) the economic impact of getting rid of cars. In her statement, she doesn't even address the real issue of the pollution. The trick is to get the audience going on another subject and hope they forget the original question.

> **REPORTER:** The issue here isn't an environmental group across the country or cars—it's the sewage your company is dumping into the river. The scientists making the charge are experienced biochemists and are concerned with children being harmed by trace chemicals in the water supply. What is your response to *that* charge?

APPEALING TO POPULAR OPINION: Assuming that because something is more popular, it's better.

> **COMPANY-EVENTS CHAIRPERSON:** I think we should go to a rap concert this year instead of having a company picnic. Rap music is very popular, so it must be good.
> **BANK PRESIDENT:** We're a bank. Most of our employees have been out of college for fifteen or more years. I don't think that many of them would give up the picnic for a rap concert.

RED HERRING: Red herrings occur when attention is drawn away from the real issue, and diverted to a side issue. The red herring is different from building a straw man. Someone builds a straw man in order to attack a side issue. Someone would use a red herring to cause others to misjudge the importance of issues. (During fox hunts, red herrings are dragged on the ground to take the dogs' minds off the foxes.)

In the following example, an insurance company is questioning a Congressman about industry legislation—he's going to try to change the subject because the bills that were promised at election time haven't materialized. He wants to divert attention from the real issue—the lack of progress.

> **INSURANCE LOBBYIST:** Congressman, during your election campaign, you promised us a bill that would allow insurance companies to open savings accounts for policyholders. Why has nothing happened?
> **CONGRESSMAN:** We are looking carefully into the matter. We're doing a study to determine if there is consumer interest in such a plan. As soon as we've completed that, we'll be moving very aggressively for passage.

Insurance companies know there is interest in the proposal. Even if there is little interest, they and their policyholders would still benefit. The Congressman has tried to divert attention away from his doing nothing to the side issue of market demand. The way to deal with a red herring is to let the herring-dragger know that you know what's going on.

> **LOBBYIST:** We all know there's a demand. Stop trying to divert us with side issues. Why the delay?

DIVIDING THE BABY: When people "divide the baby," they assume that a middle position or compromise is best. A middle position doesn't really mean each party is giving equally, or what's left will be useful. (As Peter Drucker said, "half a baby is a dead baby."[2])

> **CONTROLLER:** You've requested a $100,000 budget, and I've approved a $30,000 one. I'll meet you halfway at $65,000.
> **DEPARTMENT HEAD:** Just because $65,000 is the midpoint doesn't make it fair. I requested a $100,000 budget because that's what I need to make my department most profitable.

ARGUING BY AN EXTREME CASE: This happens when an exception to a rule is considered an obvious outcome.

> **ALICE:** I refuse to go golfing. People get hit by lightning on golf courses.
> **SHARON:** People get hit by lightning lots of places. But it won't be raining for several days, and even if it does, we can go into the clubhouse.

NOT LISTENING: People engage in "not listening" when, no matter what you say, they ignore it, giving no reasons.

> **LIZ:** That's not important.
> **SEAN:** Is there any evidence I could give you to prove my point?

If there isn't a response, then they don't want to listen, and you're wasting your time.

NEWER IS BETTER: This assumes a "new" idea is "better."

> **MARKETING DEPT:** Hey, let's give my idea a shot. It's never been tried before.
> **OPERATIONS DEPT:** Our current system is working fine. You've got great ideas, so why don't you focus them on one of our known problem areas.

THE SNOWBALL DOWN THE MOUNTAIN: This occurs when a grossly exaggerated worse-case scenario gets painted consisting of a series of events that "could happen."

> **BUREAUCRAT:** The minute we make one exception to our policies, we might as well throw out the entire employee manual.
> **SALES MANAGER:** The employee manual is a good thing to have. Having the flexibility to make decisions on a case-by-case basis only makes it stronger.

DIVERSION: Diversion occurs when words are used out of context.

> **MANUFACTURER:** Americans died for our freedom. Buying foreign products makes a mockery of their sacrifice by weakening America.
>
> **CONSUMER:** The freedom Americans died for includes the freedom to buy whatever products I want.

TRADITION: This occurs when prospects do things because they feel they should.

> **COMPANY PRESIDENT:** This company has never bought anything but Acme products.
>
> **NEW PURCHASING MANAGER:** Acme is three times more expensive than their competitors. We could be saving a fortune.

THREATS: Threats are warnings. Some kind of harm will come to the recipient of the threat when the warnings are defied.

> **CROMWELL:** My boss said that if I stop dealing with his brother, he'll fire me.
>
> **SALES REP:** (a strongly executed threat has no response) If his brother goes out of business, give me a call.

Responding to Verbal Trickery

Remember that these responses to verbal trickery are designed to keep a discussion moving and on track and not to make the party you're negotiating with feel stupid or inferior. If people inadvertently use verbal trickery or fallacious reasoning and it doesn't affect the outcome of the negotiation, allow the faulty reasoning to go unchecked to avoid damaging the negotiation.

NOTES

1. T. Edward Damer, *Attacking Faulty Reasoning* (Belmont, Calif.: Wadsworth Publishing, 1987), 1–9.
2. Peter Drucker, *The Effective Executive* (New York: Harper and Row, 1970).

Chapter 12
NEGOTIATING WITH DIFFICULT PEOPLE

Most of us tend to avoid difficult people and wind up forfeiting a relationship with them. When the prey of difficult people get home from work, dinnertime conversation can often focus on the trauma they have had to deal with that day. Antacids and sleeping aids wouldn't sell nearly as well if reality allowed us to avoid dealing with unreasonable, and sometimes hostile people. The two most popular, yet unnecessary and unproductive, methods for dealing with the difficult are avoidance and misery.

This chapter gives you a third alternative: coping. Upcoming are several tactics for dealing with difficult people, with an explanation of the causes of their behavior. Armed with the problem's cause, and a strategy for the cure, you can deal with the difficult behavior unemotionally and effectively. The descriptions of the behaviors and strategies for coping were developed using ideas from the psychological field of Transactional Analysis and from the book *Coping with Difficult People* by Robert Bramson, Ph.D.[1]

Difficult People Are Different

Before getting started, let me paint a picture of the types of difficult negotiators you're going to encounter, or may already know. Everyone has had the misfortune of needing to negotiate with someone who was ornery, mean, or abusive. If you're like most, you used the suffer or avoid techniques. Fortunately, most of us in the world are pleasant, easy to deal with, and only occasionally difficult. These strategies for dealing with abusive negotiators will rarely be needed, but will be invaluable in your negotiations arsenal.

This chapter looks at six types of difficult people you'll have to negotiate with: Sherman tanks, the super-agreeables, the know-it-all-experts, complete complainers, and exploders.[2]

The Occasionally Difficult

There's a difference between the chronically difficult and the occasionally difficult. Everyone is difficult at times. We become temporarily difficult when we're pushed beyond our limits, and when someone is really ticking us off. The general strategy for coping with the temporarily difficult is to let them vent their frustration and move on, since the behavior will be acute but short-term.

Chronically Difficult People

The chronically difficult go through life leaving a wake of destruction behind them. They're constantly making the lives of others, especially those whom they have power or authority over, trying or downright miserable. Fortunately, difficult people can be dealt with using the techniques in this chapter.

The Customer Is *Not* Always Right

An old business adage states: "The customer is always right." It has been expanded to "The boss is always right," or "The foreman is always right." (Of course, in the service, the drill sergeant *is* always right—boot camp is based on following orders, not negotiation!) Difficult people interpret variations of the saying to mean that a position of power brings them divine infallibility, no matter what the situation. I've seen patrons at McDonald's being abusive to cashiers because the 79¢ French fries were "lukewarm."

Frequently, difficult people treat others like children and punish them as such. Transactional Analysis (TA)[3] call this behavior acting like a "pig." These types of difficult people believe they're superior and feel it's their right to be verbally abusive to their "inferiors." "Pigs," not surprisingly, make the unfortunate souls whose life intersects with theirs a living hell.

Talk with the Difficult Person "Adult to Adult"

Psychologists say that when difficult people speak in an abusive manner, it is like an adult reprimanding a little child. This verbal transaction is known as a "script" because the person being abused is expected to take on the part of a child and act like one, as if he or she were in a play. (Transactional Analysis psychologists label the types of scripts difficult people enjoy playing, and develop strategies[4] for dealing with people using scripts.) Your job is to make the difficult person understand that you're not interested in being a part of his or her script by responding as an adult and not allowing the person to speak to you as a child. You take control, and force the relationship to proceed on an adult-adult level. Here's an example:

> **"PIG" NEGOTIATOR:** What the hell were you thinking when you reserved this room for the meeting? Are you stupid or don't you even have a brain?
> **CHRISTINE:** You're speaking to me like a child, which I am not. (She shouldn't address the issue of the room until the negotiator deals with her on an adult level.)

> **RATIONAL NEGOTIATOR:** My concern is that this room isn't big enough. Why was this room chosen?
> **CHRISTINE:** Though this room is a little small, it's the only one with a slide projector and a flip chart.

Those who view others as inferiors will treat them as a peer only when the relationship is forced to proceed on an adult-adult level. Interestingly, if you turn a difficult person upside down, you'll see insecurity printed on the bottom of his feet. With insecurity comes frustration and that frustration is taken out on others. The "pig" negotiator Christine had to deal with probably lashed out at her because he didn't explain his requirements clearly originally. Rather than admitting he made a mistake, he is searching for a scapegoat for the blame.

A commonality among all the techniques is reducing the insecurity difficult people feel and replacing it with permission to make mistakes and treat others with respect. Here are specific strategies for dealing with different kinds of difficult customers.

Sherman Tanks

The first type of difficult person is the Sherman tank. The Sherman tank is a hostile-aggressive individual who tries to threaten, roll over, and destroy everything in his or her path. Sherman tanks use their one-up power to threaten others far beyond what is acceptable in the normal course of business. They'll make demands far beyond what's fair. They often hold positions of importance because if they didn't, no one would bother dealing with them. People who are excessively deferent to them get drawn into their psychological script and wind up on the losing end of a lose–win deal (see chapter 9). This situation involves Bruce, a hostile-aggressive known as the "Sherman tank."[5]

BRUCE: Gee, Rich, it's a real shame the section's getting so far behind. I'm sure if you work all weekend, you'll get caught up. Give me a call on my boat if you have any questions.

RICH: I'm going away this weekend, too. Besides, early on in the project, we said we needed four engineers and three weeks to finish. Of course, we're not done yet.

BRUCE: You have two choices, finish this weekend or don't bother coming to work on Monday. See ya.

RICH: Changing plans now would ruin our weekends, and besides we're working as hard as we can.

BRUCE: It's your decision. Take it or leave it.

This is an extreme, but not uncommon, case of a "pig" engaging in a one-up power play. It's a form of blackmail called "greenmail" because the recipient will suffer financially. Negotiators often succumb to greenmail, but they cannot sustain receiving the unfair treatment. After a while they change departments, or jobs, or find new people to do business with.

If you're a sales rep and the greenmailer is a customer, you may have heard horror stories about that person or organization from others, but you think to yourself, "How difficult can they be?"

The end result is that you learn quickly that you've gotten more than you bargained for.

After Sherman tanks greenmail every coworker and supplier and no one wants to work with them or sell to them they mellow for a while and are not difficult—but usually their difficult side soon reasserts itself and the cycle begins again. Here's how to cope with the Sherman tank.

Coping with the Sherman Tank

First meet with them in person. This will allow eye contact and prevent premature closure of the meeting easily done by the Sherman tank during a phone conversation. Bruce, in the example above, was constantly trying to end the conversation and leave. The first thing Rich needs to do is to not allow Bruce to hit-and-run him. When he's done that, he's three-quarters of the way there.

RICH: Stop. Sit down, this is too important to just dump on us and then leave. Let's talk about it.

Next, he needs to explain that a healthy business relationship builds itself on a win-win strategy. Give examples of the consequences to Bruce if *his* boss were to treat *him* with one-up power plays. Finally, focus on the concerns. State the consequences to him of his causing his employees to lose and how win-lose relationships degenerate to lose-lose relationships. Develop a strategy for solving the problem without giving into threats or intimidation. Here is an example of coping with the Sherman tank.

> **RICH:** When we started the project, we estimated that it would take four engineers three weeks to complete. Is that right?
>
> **BRUCE:** Yes, but as I said before, you're running behind and need to get caught up.
>
> **RICH:** We're not running behind, we're right on schedule based on the manpower we have. I understand how you feel. Your boss wants the project accelerated. Doesn't it seem to you a little heavy-handed to be relaxing on your boat all weekend while we work? How would you feel if your boss told you to stay in the office rather than spend time at the lake because he underestimated the work force? Of course you wouldn't like it.
>
> We are trying to develop a long-term relationship with you and the company. We understand that, at times, we'll have to work especially long hours. I have several concerns. One concern in the long-term issue that apparently we need more staffing. Secondly, if the entire team needs to work this weekend, then the entire team, including you, should work. If not, I can guarantee you that some other members of the group will quit. If that happens, we'll be in a lot of trouble because it will take at least two weeks to get their replacements up to speed.
>
> **BRUCE:** All right. But I need you to tell me exactly how many hours you'll need by Monday afternoon.
>
> **RICH:** Okay. Have a good time on your boat.

When people persist in demanding more than is fair, say you can't abide by their wishes for the same reasons they wouldn't under similar circumstances—it's a win-lose deal that will ultimately become lose-lose. The Sherman tank will respect that reasoning and usually acquiesce to fairness.

If you give in, there is a certain guarantee of repeated greenmail. When "pigs" engage in one-up power plays, the difficult behavior will worsen until the win-lose situation is so out of control that the other party bails out. Hoping the difficult people will become fair or misinterpreting brief periods of adult-adult behavior as a change in character is misplaced optimism. Sherman tanks become more demanding, not less, with each "victory."

The Super-Agreeable

The super-agreeable is the person that "kills you with kindness." The super-agreeable avoids confrontations and conflict and will say anything, true or not, to keep others from getting upset. The super-agreeable may, for instance, want to hire you, but have funding fall through and put off telling you, knowing that you'll be disappointed.

A Super-Agreeable Drain

The super-agreeable will be a greater drain on your energy than the hostile-aggressive because the super-agreeable will be outwardly pleasant and the damage he or she causes is subtle. You may not even realize you're dealing with a difficult person. For example, for any number of reasons a negotiation takes an unexpected turn. The super-agreeable doesn't want to disappoint you so avoids telling you the "bad" news. He'll string you along, knowing you're not going to get what you want, telling you the project's just about ready, or he needs a few more approvals, or wants just a little more information.

> **APPLICANT:** I'm interviewing at several other companies, but don't want to accept any positions until I hear from you. I'm holding off because the career opportunities working for your department would be the best for me.
> **SUPER-AGREEABLE:** (who knows a hiring freeze has just been instituted) I've already signed the employment requisition. It just needs approval from my boss. Could you get back to me next week?
> **APPLICANT:** Sure.

Perceiving Types Aren't Difficult

The super-agreeable's delaying shouldn't be confused with Perceiving-type negotiators (chapter 6) waiting until their dominant function is addressed (chapter 8). Perceiving types are careful planners and decision makers who wait for events to occur before they'll act, which is far different from being a closure or conflict avoider. If a Perceiving type hasn't committed because he's missing a critical piece of information, he's not being difficult. He'll commit when he gets the information. Perceiving types with dominant functions of Feeling and Intuition will be the slowest to decide because Intuitives tend to want to discover all the possibilities, and Feeling types will be interested in all human impact (current and future) of the decision. When all three personality traits are present, in theory, boundless amounts of data must be weighed. In business, the expectation to make "a decision" is great. If someone's a slow decision maker, then bringing that person to closure (which is necessary for the super-agreeable, since often a decision is already made) would be viewed by the Perceiving type as being rushed into a decision—something Perceiving types dislike.

Coping with the Super-Agreeable

Listen to the customer and focus on issues as much as possible (see chapter 2). Find reasons why the super-agreeable is avoiding or delaying making a decision. If you feel the project is canceled or delayed, give them "permission" to tell you the news,[6] using "us," or "we." Here are some examples:

> **APPLICANT:** I interviewed several weeks ago. Are you sure there aren't any concerns about my background or qualifications?

> or

> **APPLICANT:** I've heard a rumor that some departments have hiring freezes. Is yours one of them?

If you don't get any response and still think you're being strung along try:

> **APPLICANT:** Why don't I call your boss directly and see if she has any questions or concerns.

> or

> **APPLICANT:** The first job I take out of college is very important because it sets the stage for future advancement. If your department does have a hiring freeze, you're actually doing me a disservice by not telling me, because other jobs that could be offered will go away. Could you check and see if that's the case?
> **SUPER-AGREEABLE:** We do have a hiring freeze going on. But I was hoping it would end and my budget would free up. If you have other opportunities out there, you should probably take one.
> **APPLICANT:** Thanks for telling me.

The super-agreeable's biggest fear is disappointing you. If you are disappointed, don't show it. This will leave the door open for future negotiations.

Know-It-All Experts

The know-it-all expert is the customer who seems to know everything about everything. There are two types of know-it-all experts, and they seek "actors" to play an important role in their scripts. The two types are the bulldozer (one who bullies others into accepting his opinion) and the balloon (the pseudo-expert). The know-it-all expert wishes others to play the part of "yes-man." If they want to curry the know-it-all expert's favor, they quickly learn to agree with everything said, and act very impressed with the knowledge of the know-it-all expert. Know-it-all experts will enjoy comfortable relationships with the yes-men in their life, although it is an alliance that is based on subservience, not on mutual respect and benefit. Also, when the know-it-all expert makes a poor decision, those in the yes-men role will be the fall-guys for not providing insights, even if those insights were not wanted.

> **KNOW-IT-ALL EXPERT:** Why didn't you tell me that all the hotels in Los Angeles were booked?
> **EMPLOYEE:** I tried, but you said you had the situation under control. (The employee is being kind. The know-it-all expert this example is based on actually said, "I don't need you telling me what to do. I was making trips to L.A. when you were in diapers.")

Know-it-all experts who are ultimate decision makers want employees who are obsequious and fawning. Know-it-all experts that aren't final decision makers act as powerfully negative forces adding unnecessary confusion and uncertainty to any negotiation. There are two types of know-it-all experts.

The Bulldozer

The first type of know-it-all expert is the bulldozer, who bullies others into agreeing (outwardly) with his opinions. More than any other type of difficult person, the bulldozer views subordinates and others as inferior and with condescension. Bulldozers try to rile things up by keeping people off-balance. They know an individual's most vulnerable position is being challenged in a group meeting. During a negotiation, the participants know they must avoid being made to look as if they are incompetent (chapter 3). Being argumentative or controversial toward a member of a group during a meeting never has a happy ending. Members of the group must show loyalty to their co-workers or bosses present at the meeting, even if they know for certain that it was their boss who was being difficult. The bulldozer works like this: Darryl introduces an idea or statement. The bulldozer makes a counterassertion. If it is a major point and Darryl says nothing he'll be viewed by some members of the group as incompetent or unknowledgeable—minimizing his credibility. Challenging the boss will force group members to take sides, dividing the group, and ultimately swaying the group away from Darryl.

Coping with the Bulldozer

Empathize with them and discover what they are getting at.

"I understand what you're saying. I've heard that idea before. Let's see if it would work in this situation."

This will inevitably lead to dismissal of the idea by the bulldozer himself because it will be apparent that his comment is unworkable. (Truly listen to the bulldozer's ideas and don't reject them out of hand because of their presentation, because some of the bulldozer's comments will be valid and useful.)

Allow the Bulldozer to Save Face

Your insightful questioning will show you as competent and knowing your business while allowing the bulldozer to save face. Ironically, the bulldozer is usually abusive to those whom he is most threatened by. If you force your knowledge on the bulldozer, you'll threaten the bulldozer even more, and the bulldozer will return an increased level of abusive behavior. Showing deference to the bulldozer (in an adult manner) will allow the bulldozer to appear competent and knowledgeable to the others. If the bulldozer's idea is rejected, it will be because you both worked the idea through and discovered it was unworkable, not because the bulldozer was ignorant. In this example, the bulldozer has just accused Bill, the head computer technician, of not doing his job properly because broken computers aren't being fixed fast enough. (Bill knows from previous meetings that the Bulldozer is an ESTJ, Extroverted, Sensing, Thinking, Judging type. He'll appeal to the bulldozer's dominant function of Thinking by doing a logical analysis of his department's policies.)

BILL: What makes you think my department isn't doing their job properly?
BULLDOZER: When computers break, no one fixes them anymore. Your people throw out the broken part and replace it with a new one. It shouldn't take more than 15 minutes to fix any system, and you have them out for days or weeks.

BILL: We do replace many component parts, you're absolutely right. The trick is to know what to replace—which isn't always readily apparent. Sometimes it takes a couple of days to run the necessary tests. But when you get your computer back it's fixed for good. Also, how many computers do you have in your department?

BULLDOZER: About one hundred.

BILL: If we stocked replacement parts for all the systems, it would cost your department three times what maintenance costs now. Sometimes we have to wait twenty-four hours to get a part shipped in from our supplier.

BULLDOZER: I didn't know that.

BILL: And you bring up another valid concern: downtime. What do you think we should do about it?

BULLDOZER: Why don't we have some loaner systems for people to use while their computers are being fixed?

BILL: We can do that.

The story above is an outstanding example of separating the person from the problem. Bill took great pride in the work and dedication of his department and deeply resented potshots being lobbed from the sidelines. You couldn't tell that from the conversation, though.

If the bulldozer sticks to his guns, it will become apparent he is a know-it-all expert to the other negotiators. They'll reject the idea behind closed doors when you're not around. Leave the idea as a possibility and allow the bulldozer's own employees to dissuade him later.

BULLDOZER: I don't care what Bill says, his department is incompetent and we should buy our maintenance contracts outside.

JACK: (one of the bulldozer's co-workers after Bill has left) Bill has done a lot of work for us. His facts are solid and his choice is logical. We won't get better service outside and it will sure cost a lot more.

The Balloon

The second type of know-it-all expert is the balloon, a pseudo-expert who seems to know everything about everything. In reality, the balloon can speak confidently about subjects he knows little or nothing about. Cliff, from the television show *Cheers*, is a balloon. Balloons are different from bulldozers in that the balloon isn't malicious. Balloons honestly believe they *are* experts. Usually they are just an annoyance, but can get meetings or sales cycles off track.

COPING WITH THE BALLOON: To cope with the balloon, carefully listen to the balloon and filter fact from fiction. This can often be difficult because balloons seem confident and often have sound arguments, although they base their conclusions on incomplete or inaccurate data. In the following example, Ron is proposing a price cut on one of his company's products. Kurt, a balloon, is throwing in his opinions about more expensive pricing being better, which, in this case, it isn't.

> **KURT:** I read that you always want to have the most expensive price because the public will assume you're the best.
> **RON:** I've heard that before, too. In fact, the *Wall Street Journal* recently had an article on status items having to be highly priced. That won't work for us, though, since we sell chalkboard erasers, which most see as a commodity item and not a status item like BMW's.

Show deference since saving face is most important to the balloon. Use phrases like, "I've heard that before, and after research we found . . ." or, "That's right, and there's more to it than that."

Assert yourself as an expert immediately. That why the balloon can show himself as an expert by agreeing with you, often citing verifiable sources like trade journals.

> **KURT:** Ron is absolutely right about that. I remember reading that article.

The Exploder

"The squeaky wheel gets the oil" is the rallying cry of the exploder. The exploder is the person who rants, raves, and attacks those whom he feels are inferior and need to be "taught a lesson."

Usually these bursts of intense anger are short-lived and they'll act reasonably after the explosion.

The exploder's script works like this: He is a cross between a child having a temper tantrum and a parent teaching a child a lesson. His "job" is to humiliate someone, while that someone's "job" is to listen quietly and feel badly. It is the ultimate form of a positional conversation, in which the exploder's position is the only one valid.

COPING WITH THE EXPLODER: Put your hand up like a traffic cop and say, "Stop." Exploders often explode because they feel threatened and yelling is their way of dealing with that emotion. Putting your hand up in this non-threatening way will get them speaking with you on an adult level. (If you point your finger at exploders, they could feel you're trying to challenge them.)

> **EXPLODER:** (at the top of his lungs) I paid good money for this and it is nothing but a piece of—
> **SALESPERSON:** (holding his hand up like a traffic cop) Stop!

 "Stop!"

> **EXPLODER:** What?
> **SALESPERSON:** I know you bought the watch from me. I know it's expensive. It's well made. Why isn't it working for you?

After the exploder has stopped exploding, give him some time to compose himself. He will usually start listening and you can speak with him on an adult-adult level and focus on issues.

The Complete Complainer

The complete complainer's glass is always half empty. These are the poor wretches who are never happy and seem to have made a hobby out of moaning about their troubles. Their complaints usually include a modicum of merit, or else no one would pay any attention. Too, the complete complainer's great problem-noticing skills may be backed up by great problem-solving skills, which remain virtually unused.

The coping strategy is to let them complain. If you've already heard that complaint before, cut them off. The complete complainer must always be directed toward a solution. And don't let them get by with a statement like, "Nothing can be done." By now you know that something can *always* be done.

> **YOU:** You've made many valid points. Now, what are we going to do about them?
> **COMPLETE COMPLAINER:** Nothing can be done. It's hopeless.
> **YOU:** You've obviously thought about this a long time. Let's examine solutions.

You'll soon find out that 1) they lack direction and you can help them, or 2) they just want to complain. By focusing the discussion on problem-solving, the complete complainer is either turned from complaining to negotiating or they walk out and find someone else to complain to.

General Coping Behavior—Conclusion

Difficult people are a fact today in all areas of life. Instead of avoiding or caving in to them, you have a third choice: coping. By labelling the behavior you have in a way depersonalized it. You'll find that this takes away much of the difficult person's ability to get on your nerves. Also, remember the underlying cause of most difficult behavior is insecurity, and defusing insecurity can go a long way toward coping.

NOTES

1. Robert Bramson, Ph.D., *Coping with Difficult People* (New York: Dell, 1983), 24–25.
2. Bramson, *Coping with Difficult People*, 37–41.
3. Eric Berne, *What Do You Say After You Say Hello?* (New York: Grove Press, 1973).
4. Berne, *What Do You Say After You Say Hello?*
5. Bramson, *Coping with Difficult People*, 14–25.
6. Eric Berne, *Games People Play* (New York: Grove Press, 1964).

Chapter 13
PERSONALITY NEGOTIATING PUTS YOU AHEAD

Now that you know about Personality Negotiating, you're ready to take what you've learned and put it to work. You may have already discovered an interesting side-effect of Personality Negotiating—you not only understand the people you work with better, but yourself, your friends, and your family, too.

Practice Makes Perfect

This book is similar to books on golfing or tennis that teach you how to improve your swing. Reading about it, golf or negotiation, may be interesting, but it is only worthwhile if you actually get out there and put what you've learned into practice. I'm sure you'll find that coming to collaborative solutions is painless and even fun.

Opening Your Eyes to Those Interesting People Around You

It's amazing to me to hear, time and time again, how thrilled Personality Negotiating seminar participants are at finally understanding their boss, their spouse, or their kids. I can usually spot them, too. They're the sleepy ones who drag themselves in on the second day. "I was up all night with my husband. I never knew that we Extroverts didn't let others speak. He thought I didn't care what he said."

Keep your eyes and ears peeled, and you'll be amazed at what you're going to notice. The person that you thought was difficult or odd really isn't after all.

I Should Know

Any good negotiator will tell you that negotiation is a learned skill and needs to be practiced. I am no exception. Several years ago, when I took my first negotiation course at Harvard, I took it because I "won" most negotiations, but not all. I figured that the course would show me what I needed to know to never "lose" a negotiation.

At the first class, the instructor said, "Why is it necessary to listen while you're negotiating?"

I volunteered without hesitation, "Because how can you attack the other party if you don't know what their positions are?"

This book is a testament to the fact that I've learned and experienced much since then. (The real answer, for those of you who like to read books backwards, is that you listen to others so that you can understand their concerns and reach collaborative solutions with them.) Now, after I teach a seminar or give a lecture, people call or write me to say that they were a little skeptical about this collaborative solution thing working, but they discovered that it does.

It sure does.

The Next Step—Set Goals

Now you're almost done. The next step is to set goals for yourself. It sounds hokey, but you also need to write those goals down. I won't harangue you with the psychological reasons why—but I'll tell you that it has something to do with the many parts of your brain working together when you write, while only a few of the parts get used when you think.

What you do is this: write down a list of five negotiations you're involved with that you want to successfully complete. Write down who they're with, what everyone's concerns are, and what needs to be done to wrap them up.

Pick two easy ones, two hard ones, and one in the middle.

Next, set a time schedule or an event schedule (depending on your Judging/Perceiving preference) to complete them by.

Finally, as Sylvester Stallone said to Mr. T in Rocky III, "Go for it!"

APPENDIX

The Negotiation Personality Guide

The Negotiation Personality guide will help you determine your own preferences and personality type. It is based on the responses of those who have attended Sales and Negotiation Training Company seminars.

DIRECTIONS: Read each of these items and circle answer **A** or **B**, depending on which response fits you best. There are no right, wrong, or better answers. You'll find information on scoring to find your personality type at the end of the test.

1. **If someone asks you a question, you usually:**
   A) reflect for a few moments, then respond.
   B) respond quickly.

2. **You are most convinced by:**
   A) a presentation with a lot of facts.
   B) a presentation with a strong overview.

3. **If you make a decision, you are usually swayed by:**
   A) how you're sure it will turn out.
   B) how you hope it will turn out.

4. **You tend to like days that are:**
   A) tightly scheduled.
   B) spontaneous.

5. **You like:**
   A) short meetings.
   B) long meetings.

6. **When learning a new concept, a lot of details first:**
   A) are essential to understanding.
   B) are overwhelming.

7. **If you are buying something for someone else, you are concerned:**
   A) that you are buying the right thing.
   B) that they will like it.

8. **When you make a significant decision, you usually:**
   A) allot yourself time to make it.
   B) take as much time as you need.

9. **You would rather go out with a few friends:**
   A) to a quiet restaurant.
   B) to a crowded party.

10. **When describing something, you usually:**
    A) describe it literally.
    B) describe it conceptually.

11. **You like dealing with people who are:**
    A) nice.
    B) predictable.
12. **When you make major purchases, they are usually:**
    A) planned.
    B) unplanned.
13. **When someone wants you to get back to them with information, you prefer:**
    A) writing them a proposal and sending it to them.
    B) meeting with them and talking about it.
14. **If someone gave you a proposal on inexpensive paper, you would:**
    A) view that negatively.
    B) probably not notice it or be bothered by it.
15. **When you buy something, you are more concerned with:**
    A) its cost.
    B) how much people will like it.
16. **If you made a bad decision, you would feel:**
    A) it was the best decision at the time.
    B) like you were rushed.
17. **You prefer being with people who are:**
    A) quiet.
    B) talk a lot.
18. **You tend to:**
    A) notice little things.
    B) not notice little things.
19. **When you think about several people with much in common, you tend to think of them:**
    A) as a group.
    B) as individuals.
20. **If you're given a deadline for making a decision, and there's not enough time, you would:**
    A) make it anyway, with the data you've got.
    B) allow the deadline to slip until you have all the data.
21. **You would rather have:**
    A) a desk in an open area.
    B) a desk off by itself.
22. **You like buying things that are:**
    A) the latest and greatest.
    B) tried and true.
23. **If you're in a negotiation and two people are arguing, you:**
    A) feel uncomfortable that there is disharmony.
    B) assume that interpersonal conflict is unavoidable.

24. **You've just made a big decision. You are most likely:**
    A) worried it wasn't the right thing to buy.
    B) relieved the decision is over.
25. **You find your most tiring days to be:**
    A) days when you meet many new people.
    B) days when you are alone.
26. **You think untried, new ideas are:**
    A) interesting and useful.
    B) sometimes interesting, but often unworkable.
27. **If your company has a layoff that you know is going to be financially difficult for some employees, you would:**
    A) feel bad for those being laid off.
    B) assume that layoffs are unfortunate, but inevitable.
28. **If you overloaded your appointment schedule one day, you would:**
    A) try to reschedule some of the appointments.
    B) try to keep all the appointments, even if it was difficult.
29. **If there is a long period of silence during a conversation, it is your inclination to:**
    A) fill it in.
    B) use it to think.
30. **When you make a decision, you most want to know:**
    A) how it fits into future plans.
    B) how it benefits you immediately.
31. **If someone complains about you boss, you would:**
    A) take it personally.
    B) not take it personally.
32. **You think it's important to have a:**
    A) general sense of time.
    B) concrete sense of time.
33. **You prefer:**
    A) introducing yourself to someone.
    B) having someone introduce you.
34. **You are swayed more by how:**
    A) concepts relate to facts.
    B) facts relate to concepts.
35. **After trying with no luck to make disgruntled people happy, you would:**
    A) keep trying until you are successful.
    B) give up.
36. **You're usually:**
    A) late.
    B) on time.

37. **If a phone call has to be made, you would prefer:**
    A) having someone else make it.
    B) making it yourself.
38. **When faced with a new problem with no predetermined rules and regulations, you would:**
    A) work within the rules established for other company programs, using accepted company procedures.
    B) think of as many solutions to the problem as possible, despite the established rules.
39. **Your best buying decisions were made:**
    A) rationally and precisely.
    B) emotionally.
40. **When you buy something with several options:**
    A) you decide when you're comfortable that you have enough information.
    B) you set up a deadline for making a final decision, and then work to get all the information by that deadline.
41. **When you leave a room after a spirited discussion, you are more likely to think:**
    A) why didn't I say something?
    B) why did I say that?
42. **You prefer to think of yourself as a:**
    A) pragmatist.
    B) dreamer.
43. **You tend to be a person who makes decisions that are:**
    A) consistent.
    B) based on extenuating circumstances.
44. **If you came to a fork in the woods, you would take:**
    A) the road less travelled.
    B) the road more travelled.

SCORING:
INTROVERT/EXTROVERT SCALE
Add the **A** answers for questions
1, 5, 9, 13, 17, 37, 41
Add the **B** answers for questions
21, 25, 29, 33

Put the Total here:＿＿＿＿＿ I/E

If the Total is 6 or more you're most likely an **Introvert**; otherwise you're most likely an **Extrovert**.

SENSING/INTUITIVE SCALE
Add the **A** answers for questions
2, 6, 10, 14, 18, 28, 42
Add the **B** answers for questions
22, 26, 30, 34

Put the Total here:_____ **S/N**

If the Total is 6 or more you're most likely a **Sensing** type; otherwise you're most likely an **Intuitive** type.

THINKING/FEELING SCALE
Add the **A** answers for questions
3, 7, 15, 19, 39, 43
Add the **B** answers for questions
11, 23, 27, 31, 35

Put the Total here:_____ **T/F**

If the Total is 6 or more you're most likely a **Thinking** type; otherwise you're most likely a **Feeling** type.

JUDGING/PERCEIVING SCALE
Add the **A** answers for questions
4, 8, 12, 16, 20
Add the **B** answers for questions
24, 28, 32, 36, 40, 44

Put the Total here:_____**J/P**

If the Total is 6 or more you're most likely a **Judging** type; otherwise you're most likely a **Perceiving** type.

NOTE: This is *not* the Myers-Briggs Type Indicator and it is not intended to be a substitute for the MBTI. This guide, designed to determine negotiation personality, is based on responses of attendees during Sales and Negotiation Training Company's negotiation and sales seminars.

INDEX